THE HOME PORT

BOOTLE, THE BLITZ AND THE BATTLE OF THE ATLANTIC

Bull Information Systems Limited supports the work of Sefton Metropolitan Borough Council and is privileged to be the principal sponsor of this project.

THE HOME PORT

BOOTLE, THE BLITZ AND THE BATTLE OF THE ATLANTIC

by

BRYN MARSH and SUE ALMOND

SEFTON COUNCIL

METROPOLITAN BOROUGH OF SEFTON
EDUCATION DEPARTMENT

Additional Material
and Interviews:

Lucy Parker and Ann Stevens

ACKNOWLEDGEMENTS

Paul Kemp, *Imperial War Museum*

Margaret Procter, *Merseyside Record Office*

Jenny Kermode, *University of Liverpool*

Captain H Mucklow, RN, *Naval Regional Officer*

Susan Goodfield, *National Museums and Galleries on Merseyside*

Richard New, *Bull HN Information Systems*

Education Department

John Marsden, Director

John Allen

Harry Brocklebank

Simon Kensdale

Liz Mills

Tony Powell

Sheila Ramsay

Linda Rimmer

Terry Roose

Chief Executive's Department

Graham Haywood, Chief Executive

Danny Dutton

Elaine Jones

Tom Walsh

Sefton Library Services

Jenny Stanistreet

Andrew Farthing

And particularly Janet Vicary for her endless patience in typing out the many drafts of this book.

Photographs courtesy of Imperial War Museum, Sefton Libraries, the National Museums and Galleries on Merseyside, and Mrs. Jean Brown.

BJM & SA

ISBN No. 0 9521312 0 X

Design and layout: Pheon Graphics, Southport
Phototypesetting: Andow Studios, Southport
Reprographics: Almond Jones Ltd., Liverpool
Print: Albion, Kirkby, Liverpool

CONTENTS

FOREWORD

by

JOE BENTON, JP, MP for BOOTLE

This is a book which needed to be written and I commend Sefton Council, and particularly Bryn Marsh and Sue Almond for all their hard work. Bootle and Litherland suffered more than any other comparable communities in the Blitz: more disruption, more damage to houses and more deaths per head of population. During the war news of the sufferings of Merseyside were suppressed for reasons, no doubt sound, of national security. After the war, minds inevitably concentrated on the future and reconstruction and somehow the story of our war never came to be written down.

It is fitting that the story of Bootle's war should be linked to the commemoration of the 50th Anniversary of the Battle of the Atlantic. Bootle was the Home Port for the convoy escorts and for many of the merchantmen. Most Bootle families had a connection with the sea or the docks and sometimes both.

This book has brought back many memories for me and caused me to re-examine my own roots. I suspect it will cause many others to do the same.

When war broke out I was six years old. My father was a docker and we lived in a rented house in Keir Hardie Avenue. Eventually, I was to have eight brothers and one sister. I can still recall vividly episodes from my wartime childhood.

I remember my mother's anguished uncertainty over whether she should allow us to be evacuated. After talking it over with the Headteacher of St Monica's Infant School she decided, much to my relief, to keep us at home. The war was quite unreal for me until the first raid when six of us had to huddle under the stairs. Eventually we had our own Anderson shelter and air raids became quite an adventure with little sleep and a pile of old "Beanos", "Dandys" and "Radio Fun" to read. I can recall though, my own nagging fears and my mother's concern for my father's safety when he was on the night shift at the Docks. The war at least brought him some security of employment and a temporary halt to the humiliating uncertainties of the early morning queue for "hire" at the Dock gate. Despite his regular wage, I can still remember hunger and want for basic necessities. Whatever the textbooks of the war say, basic supplies did run out, at least in Bootle. On some days there was simply no bread in the shops however long you queued - of course as the eldest lad in the family, queuing was one of my responsibilities.

The people of Bootle survived the hardship and devastation of the war at least in part because they were already used to fighting for survival. The 1930s Depression had been a desperate time for most of the Borough's people. Strong family ties, good neighbours and the practical and spiritual help of the Church, however, provided us with a real sense of community and of belonging. Bootle survived the war because its people could look out for each other.

As I reflect back on that time I can see now that the whole direction of my life was heavily influenced by my pre-war and wartime childhood. For me, political principles have to be rooted in Christian principles. We have a duty to look after our neighbour and we have to recognise that both poverty and war are evil.

I hope that those who read this book will recognise both the good and the evil inherent in the story of this conflict. Many suffered and many died during the war. We have another duty and that is of simple remembrance. The 50th Anniversary of the Battle of the Atlantic will be commemorated in Bootle on May 28th 1993. The last extracts in this book are from letters written by a German U-boat Commander. It is appropriate to repeat his words in recollection of the day when his submarine sank a British Destroyer:

> "a date for me to memorise this terrible bloody war and to feel with all the wives, parents and children mourning for a beloved life."

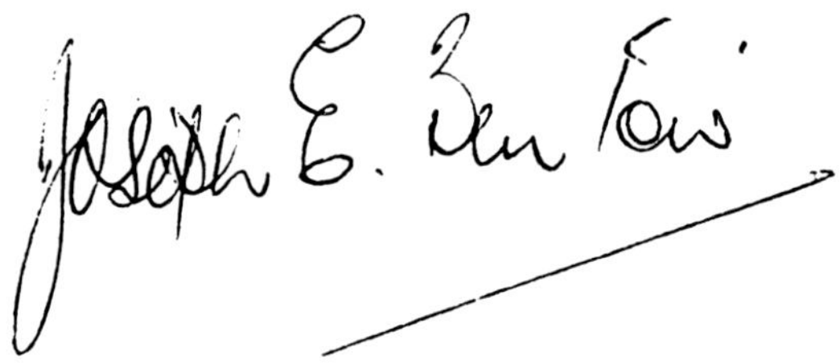

JOE BENTON

INTRODUCTION

House of Commons : 9 April 1941

Winston Churchill:

"But after all everything turns upon the Battle of the Atlantic which is proceeding with growing intensity on both sides. Our losses in ships and tonnage are very heavy and, vast as our shipping resources which we control, these losses could not continue indefinitely without seriously affecting our war effort and our means of subsistence.

Where are we to find another three or four million tons to fill the gap which is being created and carry us on through 1942? We are building merchant ships upon a very considerable scale and to the utmost of our ability having regard to other calls upon our labour. We are also making a most strenuous effort to make ready for sea the large number of vessels which have been damaged by the enemy. We are doing our utmost to accelerate the turn round of our ships, remembering - and this is the striking figure - that even 10 days saved on the turn round of our immense fleets is equal to a reinforcement of 5,000,000 tons of imports in a single year.

The Battle of the Atlantic must, however, be won not only in the factories and shipyards but upon blue water. I am confident that we shall succeed in coping with the air attacks which are made upon the shipping in the Western Approaches. But while I am hopeful that we shall gain mastery over the air attack upon our shipping, the U-boats ranging ever further to the Westward constitute a menace which must be overcome if the life of Britain is not to be endangered.

Once we have gained the Battle of the Atlantic, however far Hitler may go or whatever new millions and scores of millions he may lap in misery, then it is sure that, armed with the sword of retributive justice we shall be on his track."

Berlin Sportpalast : 30 January 1941

Adolf Hitler:

"Whoever thinks he can help England should know that every ship, with or without escort, that comes within range of our torpedo tubes, will be torpedoed.

At sea U-boat warfare will begin this spring, and they will notice here, too, that we have not been asleep. Production has been enormously increased in all fields. The year 1941 will be the historic year of the establishment of a great new order in Europe. Our belief and confidence is that we shall achieve victory. Let our prayer be that God may not forsake us in the struggle of the coming year."

The War in the Western Approaches

The chapters of this book seek to explore the impact of world war on a town and on its people and, in particular, examine the human cost of that extraordinary and protracted naval campaign called "The Battle of the Atlantic". "The Battle

(opposite)
Royal visit to Bootle in 1940 to view bomb damaged areas.
(top, courtesy Jean Brown)
(below, Sefton Libraries)

of the Atlantic" was not a battle but a campaign of great complexity that lasted the length of the Second World War from 1939 to 1945. The preliminary round had been fought from 1916 to 1918 in the First World War and the British Isles, starved of the essentials of life by the German campaign of submarine warfare, had been close to defeat. That war was won and lost in Atlantic waters as well as in Flanders mud. In the second round, particularly from 1939 to 1943 Britain again faced defeat by strangulation of its supply line through the "Western Approaches" to the United Kingdom ports.

It was Winston Spencer Churchill, inevitably, who coined the phrase by which the great campaign became known "The Battle of the Atlantic", and this is defined elsewhere. The phrase, sonorous, and memorable in its impact, distorts however, the reality of the long and deadly war for control of the sea. More telling is Churchill's less oratorical but far more revealing comment after the great struggle was over, "... the only thing that ever really frightened me during the war was the U-boat peril".

This book then has a unique perspective on the Battle of the Atlantic: it examines aspects of the war in the context of the home port. After 50 years, the fascination of the war in the Western Approaches remains, because there were so many elements at play. The war at sea both in the first and second round was, at heart, a technical war fought over great distances. In every other field of the titanic struggle now called the Second World War, the majority of campaigns were fought between more or less competent combatants having the same military aims and comparable military strategies - tank for tank, plane for plane. Cities were bombed on both sides. But in the Western Approaches like did not fight like. The struggle was between submarine and surface ship for control, not of the sea itself, but of the supply lines to the British Isles.

Despite the advanced technical nature of the overall campaign, it was fought in the intensely hostile environment of the Atlantic by small numbers of men in very vulnerable ships and submarines. The greatest number of casualties occurred amongst merchant sailors - technically non-combatants. In addition, from 1940, the war at sea became also a battle for the home ports. In particular the port of Liverpool was essential to the supply of the whole British mainland and hence the entire war effort - and the great "Liverpool" docks were in Bootle. Not only that: Bootle provided many of the dockers and many of the seamen. It was estimated that, prior to the Second World War, two out of three households had a direct or indirect employment connection with either the port or the Royal or Merchant Navies. Bootle was at the heart of the home port and the Gladstone Dock channel was the great artery. The convoy escort groups sailed from Bootle and were adopted as Bootle's own. The German air raids on Bootle were intended to destroy the docks and hinterland, cutting the vital supply line at its base.

THE DOCKS

The Great Northern Docks

The Atlantic War was a war for the supply lines, and particularly for the northern sea route from the United States and Canada to the United Kingdom. But control of the sea routes alone was never enough. The ports on both sides of the Atlantic were an integral part of the war. Problems of harbour congestion as the convoys assembled were severe enough in the main export docks at New York and Halifax, Nova Scotia to hamper the war effort and in Britain the capacity of the docks and their vulnerability to air attack became a crucial factor in the outcome of the war.

The Caesar class fleet destroyer *HMS Carron*, outside the Gladstone docks taking up its station as an escort to the famous liner, *Mauretania* - a wartime troop ship *(Imperial War Museum)*

Two great river ports had traditionally handled the New World trade, the Mersey and, to a lesser extent, the Clyde. In the 1870s the Mersey Docks and Harbour Board, facing the threat to trade from Glasgow and London, and to corporate pride because of Manchester's plans to become a port by means of a canal, turned its attention to "... a grand scheme of northern deep docks". A Board member said:

"What we need are deep water entrances coming from the sea on the Lancashire side and then we shall have surrounded our difficulties."

The result was Langton Dock, opened in 1879. Until Langton's own lock was ready, the connecting waterways with the original Bootle Dock - the Brocklebank - had to be used, but when the dock complex was complete, the port was able to reassert its pre-eminence and cater for the new breed of large trans-atlantic grain ships. Within a few years, however, the Board was under threat again, this time from the great passenger shipping lines culminating in the ultimate threat from the doyen of the passenger lines - Cunard. Cunard issued an ultimatum: unless Liverpool could berth the greatest liners, the entire operation of the line would be moved to another port. The port authorities moved with uncharacteristic speed and commissioned a design for new docks which matched in grandeur those of Jesse Hartley for the Albert Dock, but on a vaster scale. The result was the Gladstone Dock, which could take the great passenger liners, but could also shelter the new improved "Dreadnought" battleships. The first stage of the dock was opened in 1914 by King George V with Queen Mary and the future Edward VIII, and was named after Robert Gladstone, the Chairman of the Board. War intervened and the Bootle docks were not completed until 1921. The complete system however, still, represents one of the world's great harbour systems comprising in total the Brocklebank, Langton, Alexandra, Hornby and Carriers docks, plus "branch" docks and the Gladstone itself. The latter consists of a massive river entrance lock 1,070 feet long and 130 feet wide and a main pool of 25 acres, capable of "turning" the longest ships. But the key to its success lies in the lock system, and in the transit sheds on the north side which enabled ships to load and discharge afloat. These two elements were crucial in the Second World War, together with the efficient rail system feeding into the port.

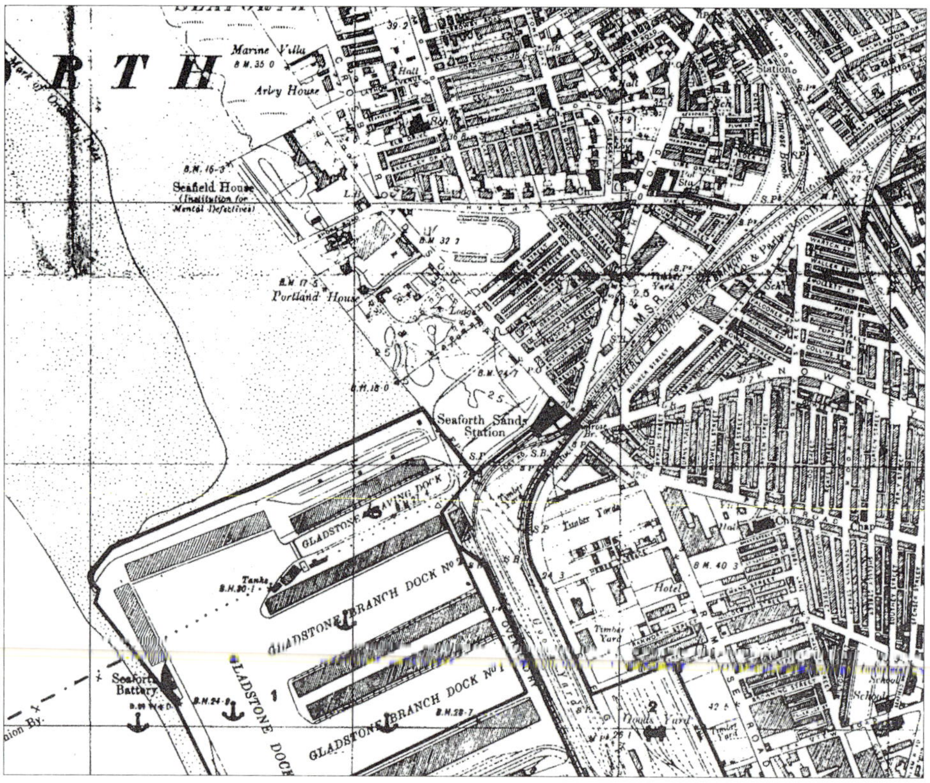

German Luftwaffe map of the Bootle docks - the targets are indicated by the darker shaded areas. The map is a copy of an Ordnance Survey map.

Preparation for War in the Docks

Industrial relations in the dock industry were appalling. Relative peace in the 1930s was secured only by the Depression, and ever-present threat of unemployment with relief barely at subsistence levels. There was no security of employment for any docker. Each morning the workforce queued afresh at the dock gates - each day's work at the whim of the overseer.

The rest of the United Kingdom was, however, dependent on the docks for survival in times of war. In this area at least, there was early Government recognition of the risks associated with failure to plan for imports and speedy turn around of ships under war conditions. To these specific ends, a Port Emergency Committee (PEC) was established in 1936 and was given extensive powers in the event of war. These powers included the compulsory removal of goods and levying of penalty rents, determining the number of dockers to be employed on a ship, and suspending cargo checking operations, such as sorting, weighing and customs examination. The Government stopped short of addressing the main issue, which was the way dockers were employed. When war started in August 1939, the docks, crucial to the survival of the country, were still being manned by an alienated workforce employed on a casual basis. The PEC could not override statute or by-laws without reference to the Minister of War Transport and nor could it employ workers directly.

The PEC, within the limits of its powers, acted with commendable vigour and there was genuine co-operation with the Bootle Borough Council. The St John's Ambulance Brigade was used to train salaried staff as first aid operators and they, in turn, were required to train a set number of other workers in basic techniques. Throughout the docks First Aid posts, air raid shelters and decontamination centres (preparations for gas attacks were a legacy of the Great War) were established. Protective clothing and respirator stores were designated and a full scale camouflage painting programme was started. "Blackout" proved to be an impossible problem to solve. The docks needed lights for safety purposes and for essential night-time working within the freight sheds. Pre-war experiments with reduced lighting caused a 50% reduction in speed of handling goods, which was only partly alleviated by the issue of hand-lamps to dockers.

The Docks at War

After the fall of France in 1940, the port of London ceased to be an effective conduit for international trade. German control of the French coast and mines laid by both sides made the English Channel far too dangerous for large-scale enshipment. While the East coast route to London was still used riskily for collier convoys from the North East, the Mersey Dock estate now became the keystone of national survival handling all other essential commodities.

In July 1940 the first air attack on the Docks came; Churchill summed it up:

"It would seem that this problem constitutes the most dangerous part of our whole front."

One dock gateman recalls standing on the roof of a dock building during a raid watching the docks burning in both directions:

"Bombs would whistle and scream through the air. Incendiaries fell and burst all over the place. There was no question of you going into a shelter and leaving the gate unmanned. You had to wait until someone relieved you. You'd go on at 4.00 in the afternoon, a raid would start so you wouldn't get relieved until 6.00 the following morning. There was no overtime, just a flat rate of pay. We worked shifts: 8.00 am - 4.00 pm, 4.00 pm - 11.00 pm or 11.00 pm - 8.00 am for seven days a week. We'd swap shifts on a Saturday, we'd finish at 4.00 pm and start nights at 11.00 the same day."

He also recalls the insistence on blackout that followed the first raid and the farcical horror of falling into a dock in pitch darkness. This was an experience shared by many others - mainly sailors leaving the notorious Flotilla Club on the Gladstone Dock side, but also a Bootle emergency ambulance in 1944. Raids continued intermittently with serious damage occurring in December 1940. The climax came in that series of destructive raids in May 1941 known throughout

Merseyside as "the May Blitz". The Chairman of the Mersey Docks and Harbour Board described the results:

"The whole way from Gladstone to Sandon, inclusive there are no entrances working. Brocklebank Dock is blocked off and ships are locked in. The overhead railway is down in several places. If we can get the obstruction at the Canada Dock removed we shall be able to work our dock lines through. We are very helpless in the meantime as there are no railway stations open to receive dock headed traffic although some are receiving carted traffic."

One half of the 144 berths on the Dock estate were taken out of action, plus vast quantities of goods still in the berthed ships or in the warehouses on the dockside.

Even before the great May raids of 1941 the crisis in the docks acted as a spur to radical changes in their management. Churchill had already made his views known on the effect of delays in a directive on 6 March 1941, insisting that something had to be done to reduce the terrible slowness of the turnround of ships in British ports, "... a saving of 15 days in this process would be in itself the equivalent of 5 million tons of imports". The result was a speeding-up of the process of "nationalisation", not of the docks themselves but of the dock workers who now came under the direct control of the Minister of Transport. Coupled with this, thousands of men with trade skills were released from the armed forces to help clear 800,000 tons of shipping awaiting repair. Merseyside dockers would receive security of employment for the first time and a guaranteed minimum wage (£4 2s 6d for 11 "turns").

According to Ernest Bevin, Minister of Labour and National Service, "... transport was the key to victory and its effective organisation would shorten the war. It lay largely in the hands of ship and port authorities and men whether the U-boat menace was mastered".

1941, Gladstone Docks: The Prime Minister touring the dock area. The contemporary press release says: "Alluding to their well filled plates he asked "Are you managing to get plenty of food?" "Aye sir, we are doing grand, thank you", was the reply". A somewhat implausible exchange. *(Imperial War Museum)*

On 13 March 1942, a radical proposal was made by the North West Regional Port Director. Merseyside dockers were released from all wartime working restrictions. Dockers would be "left free for a trial period to work in any zone or for any employer preferred and to discipline themselves for a week on the "honour" principle, suspensions and punishments being dropped, if successful the system would be continued". In the context of the previous 70 years of management/union warfare this was a revolutionary announcement. The scheme was a success and was continued. This is not to say that industrial peace and harmony reigned supreme during the war, simply that the importance of key workers in a time of danger and of labour shortage tilted the balance of relationship between employer and employee for the first time in the latter's favour. It has to be a matter of regret that after the war employment reverted to its pre-war pattern and industrial relations descended to a new level of bitterness and bloody- mindedness.

The air campaign against the Mersey Docks and the consequent destruction of much of the Borough of Bootle was essentially a secret war. Bootle and the other Merseyside districts were rarely mentioned in the national press or on radio. At best there might be cryptic references: "... heavy air raids took place last night, a northern port was the target, there were some casualties". Between air raids the routine of the port ground on; the unremitting hard labour, long shifts and a permanent sense of impending chaos as the river jammed up with ships waiting for free berths. Daily conferences took place with the dock masters to discuss ship management and cargo priority and the rapid servicing of the Royal Navy escorts. It was not until the advent, in 1942, of the free-ranging naval support groups that there was any sense of excitement in the docks. It is not possible now to capture the sheer sense of adventure that these fighting ships brought into the Gladstone Dock and Bootle in contrast to the grim, rationed existence of the first three years of the war. The support groups had their submarine kills emblazoned on black skull and crossbone flags, their crews had the unofficial freedom of the Borough and the ships and their exploits were avidly supported.

While the docks gave sanctuary to naval heroes, their real significance can be read in the hard statistics of the war: 75,000,000 tons of goods handled, 91 acres of dockland damaged, 91 ships damaged or sunk within the dock basins, and 68 separate bombing raids on the port and its environs.

1945:
Crew of a Captain's class frigate in Gladstone Dock. Five U-boats is their claimed total of kills. Crossed scalpels at the bottom left indicate two surgical operations performed at sea during patrols. The key is the support group's sign.
(Imperial War Museum)

BOOTLE

Pre-War Bootle

In the early 19th century Bootle was an attractive little health resort, a desirable residential area for the burgeoning middle class in nearby Liverpool. Bootle's growth followed in the wake of its prosperous neighbour, and Borough status was granted in 1869. The population trebled during the great period of Dock construction between 1881 and 1921, reaching its inter- war peak of over 82,000 in 1922 before settling at about 74,000 the year before the start of the Second World War. Much of this increase resulted from the migration of large numbers of Welsh and Irish, seeking employment in the building of the docks, railways and in the related industries of the town. The social character of the town changed dramatically to that of a predominantly working class urban environment. One thing remained consistent throughout Bootle's history: the town was ***not*** part of Liverpool and all subversive attempts at a take-over were resolutely resisted. The Liverpool bid through Act of Parliament in 1903 to incorporate Bootle within its boundaries was defeated to great public rejoicing.

During the inter-war years Bootle, in common with all northern industrial towns, suffered from problems of chronic unemployment and pervasive poverty, with the pool of unemployed labour serving to push down the wages of those in work. There was no universal welfare provision and while the Boards of Guardians with their powers of committal to the dreaded workhouses (Walton in the case of Bootle residents), had been abolished in 1929, all benefits were still savagely means-tested by the local authority Public Assistance Committees which replaced them. The stable employment prospects of the merchant fleet and dock labouring, where son traditionally followed father into employment, had suffered the consequences of international economic decline. Unemployment was long term and structural. Casual labour was the order of the day, epitomised by the queues at the Dock gates at dawn.

Housing conditions were dismal, particularly in the immediate vicinity of the docks. The facts make for grim reading. In the mid 1930s the Council found that a fifth of the municipal housing stock was overcrowded, or provided accommodation for their inhabitants deemed to be unsatisfactory. The reports on housing conditions galvanised the Borough Aldermen and a rigorous Council administration under Partington, the Town Clerk, took major steps to alleviate these problems. By 1939 the original overcrowding problem had been reduced by a third. Nevertheless, more than 370 families were still waiting to be housed and more than 40% of the municipal houses inspected were found to be verminous, and over 10% were structurally defective and potentially unsafe. At the start of the war there were approximately 17,000 houses in the town, in an

(opposite)
Residents of Worcester Road, Bootle, surveying the damage to their homes the morning after an air raid.
(Sefton Libraries)

area of approximately 2400 acres, the area of the Docks being the most densely populated: a classic northern scene of narrow cobbled streets and terraced houses. The Borough's health record was very poor. The birth rate was one-third higher than the national average during the 1930s, its infant mortality rate was even higher. The establishment of the first health centre in 1932 was aimed at relieving some of the health problems of the poor, of course, it was established by the Borough Council and not by national government. The Borough's Medical Officer of Health, Dr F Wood, reported in 1938 that Council action had eradicated "the major 19 epidemic diseases" and that no deaths had occurred in the previous year from typhoid fever and cholera, despite the proximity of the port. Yet the epidemics which did occur were bad enough: 20 deaths from measles, 17 deaths from diptheria and 97 from pneumonia in 1938, plus a steady stream caused by bronchitis, TB and whooping cough - many of them young children. Child health statistics were appalling: 20% of children were reported to have rickets, (including 27% of 2 year olds), while almost 20% of children suffered from skin and scalp diseases, subnormal nutrition and anaemia.

Bootle was a poor borough and the lives of the majority of its people were unremittingly hard. There were some compensations. Family ties were strong, and the extended family provided real support across both the generations and through the network of cousins and more distant relatives. Strong religious links helped to support communities. Real poverty and desperation afflicted mostly those who fell outside these voluntary networks. There was also a strong sense of civic pride and loyalty. In the 1930s the Borough Council made vigorous attempts to revitalise the town, looking back to its 19th century past as a holiday resort. The parks and recreation grounds were redeveloped - North, South and Derby Parks were modernised, incorporating children's paddling pools and model boating lakes; Stuart Road playing fields, golf links, and a sports stadium were constructed. Attempts were made to renew housing stock and acquisition of new land had been planned for housing estates. By 1939 the monthly unemployment figures were less than half that of nine years earlier - the fall was due, in equal measure, to a general economic upturn, war preparations and the impact of civic works.

Preparation for War in Bootle

In 1937, as unease about German intentions spread, the Government issued notification to local authorities of the requirement for "a scheme of air raid precautions in the event of war with Germany". Bootle Borough Council minutes show that the Bootle Aldermen responded with enthusiasm. The Air Raid Precautions (ARP) Emergency Committee met for the first time in January 1938, and a First World War veteran, Major George Salt, was appointed Air Raid Precautions Officer for the Borough. Bootle's Civil Defence Scheme, which was to remain more or less intact throughout the war period, was forwarded to central Government early the following year. The scheme showed evidence of careful planning and a high degree of intelligent foresight. Clearly much of this was due to Major Salt himself who created a structure which lasted throughout the war and to Harold Partington, the Town Clerk, who cut across rigid 1930s bureaucratic procedures with enormous enthusiasm. (Partington's proudest moment came in the war when he was given his own Lee-Enfield rifle.)

The former British Oxygen Company building in Knowsley Road was purchased with £13,000 of Government aid, for conversion to ARP Headquarters. It was considered by the Home Office to be the best all-round headquarters in the country, with its accessible, central position, its administration block, equipment and clothing store for anti-gas gear and other essentials of the various civil defence services, its rescue and decontamination depot, and facilities for emergency vehicles. Critically as events were to prove, the Headquarters had its own supply of potable water from one of the few known wells in the Borough. When modern pumping equipment was installed it was estimated 100 gallons of water per minute could be drawn.

Arrangements were made for all services required for the defence of the Borough and the preservation of life in the event of attack. The Library basement in the Town Hall complex was converted and reinforced to become a Report and Control Centre. The Centre was staffed 24 hours a day. Here notification of potential air raids was received and orders given by telephone to sound the six sirens throughout the Borough. A watching post was set up on the roof of the Headquarters, with a back-up in the church tower of St Robert Bellarmine. In case telephone lines were disconnected a Messenger Service was established, consisting of teenagers from various youth organisations - Air Training Corps, Sea and Army Cadets, Girls' Training Corps, Girls' Junior Air Corps, and the Boy Scout Association. The Scouts provided particularly consistent service and received a Silver Cross for their work during the Blitz.

1940:
The Brecknock Battalion, South Wales Borderers, exercising in Bootle. Officers have just held a roadside conference.
(Imperial War Museum)

Arrangements were made for the evacuation of school children, expectant mothers, children below the age of five years accompanied by their mothers, and the aged, blind and infirm, in accordance with the Government-sponsored scheme.

Extensive casualty treatment services based at the Health Centre, Knowsley Road, and at the Outpatients' Department of Bootle General Hospital, Derby Road, were organised and necessary equipment obtained. The General Hospital was effectively abandoned shortly after the outbreak of war because its proximity to the Docks made it a dangerous location. The main emergency centre was then established at Linacre Infectious Diseases Hospital with a capacity to cope with 40 - 50 emergency patients per night. This was intended to be a staging hospital with patients transferred to nearby hospitals the following day. One mobile first aid post was also used, although this was found to have limited effectiveness. Staff for emergency duties were drawn primarily from the St John's Ambulance Service, which was much expanded in preparation for war and linked with the Dock's casualty planning arrangements. The Council had received instruction from the Government that the Ambulance Service should consist half of drivers and half of attendants. In a relatively poor borough such as Bootle few people had driving licences and it proved difficult to recruit drivers. Eventually, it was accepted that instruction would be given to women and they became the majority of ambulance drivers. Bootle Constabulary's prison van was commandeered for their driving lessons.

841 Air Raid Wardens were recruited, both full-time and voluntary workers. The Service Headquarters were situated at the Central Police Station, with the wardens staffing numerous posts throughout the Borough both day and night. On Major Salt's initiative, rescue parties were also established for the task of releasing those trapped and injured from damaged buildings. Recruits for this service were drawn mainly from the Council's Public Works and Engineers Sections, because of their expertise in building construction. Similarly, staff of the Street Cleansing Department of the Borough were employed in the Decontamination Squads, required to cleanse contaminated buildings, streets and materials in the event of a gas attack. The one area where Major Salt underestimated the difficulties was in coping with the dead. At the height of the Blitz local undertakers could not manage and this was one service for which there was a dearth of volunteers. Initially the staff from Balliol Road Baths were conscripted but when they objected, the Council had to hire mortuary attendants from Manchester.

The existing Fire Service was expanded to include an Auxiliary Fire Service, with additional fire pumps and hoses supplied by the Government. Three dams were built in the Leeds-Liverpool Canal to provide reservoirs of water for fire fighting and to prevent flooding in the event of the canal being damaged. Streets were patrolled for incipient fires and two boats were converted into fire floats for use in the docks - the *Kanda*, renamed the *Simon Mahon*, after the renowned Alderman; and another named the *James Spence*, after the Mayor.

Air Raid Precautions Civil Defence personnel on the permanent staff were required to work 12 hour shifts, with one day off every seven days - a 72 hour week. One day's leave was allowed for every month of service, a maximum of 12 in a year. It was clearly a tremendous strain on those involved during the 18 months that Bootle was under attack: long periods of boredom and inactivity interspersed with violent raids.

Bootle established the first Women's Voluntary Service (WVS) for civil defence in the North West. There were over 2,000 volunteers who provided an invaluable service, particularly by staffing the mobile canteens donated by various individuals and organisations from as far afield as Canada and the United States. One such vehicle was lost when it plunged into the Alexandra Dock during a blackout - its WVS occupants were saved.

Groups of Fire Guards were set up in strategic locations particularly business premises. Local volunteers were trained by Air Raid Wardens in methods of fire control. Bootle also had its contingent of Home Guard. There were two battalions - the 77th took responsibility for defence of the town in general, and the 88th guarded factory areas and works deemed of national importance.

(above)
1941: Bootle County Hall, Pembroke Road, seriously damaged during an air raid. Note the helmet placed on the wall. *(Sefton Libraries)*

(left)
1940:
The defences of Merseyside at Fort Crosby. The fort was manned by the 77th Heavy Battery, RA, who are seen firing a four inch gun. It was only fired once in anger - and then by mistake.
(Imperial War Museum)

The Army's anti-aircraft battery was housed at the Stadium sports ground, with living quarters erected on the municipal golf course. A RAF barrage balloon unit made its headquarters at Derby Park bowling green. Several of the balloons were to break loose, one damaging the roof of St Mary's Church as the spire was hit.

Mutual aid schemes were devised across the North West region, to ensure assistance between local authorities in the event of attack. It seems though that the old antipathies died hard. Bootle was extremely reluctant to enter into a mutual aid agreement with the real enemy - Liverpool. Local brigades were reluctant to cross borders and rivalries between the respective fire brigades caused a scandal. This situation was a prime cause of the establishment of the National Fire Service on May 13, 1941, which removed fire brigades from local authority control until 1948.

The process of establishing and training the necessary civil defence personnel was a complex one. At times Major Salt clearly felt frustrated in his efforts by constant alterations to regulations and to the authorised numbers of personnel, by both central Government and the Regional Commission. Numerous items of equipment were requisitioned or otherwise obtained, including such things as shovels, haversacks, overalls, helmets and over one hundred and fifty thousand sandbags, as well as 1500 babies' anti-gas helmets.

The public air raid shelter was effective. Damage is minor considering an HE bomb fell within a few feet of it. *(Sefton Libraries)*

All road signs to the Mersey Tunnel and other places were removed by May 1940 and road blocks established in the outlying areas of the town (although the chances of Hitler invading by way of Bootle were rather remote). Coupled with the blackout the result at first was close to chaos. Foreign aliens were registered in accordance with the Aliens (Protected Areas) Order 1940 and of 176 reporting to the Police, 107, comprising 20 nationalities, were allowed to remain. A number of Germans, Italians and Austrians were required to leave the district.

Blackout exercises were undertaken, the lighting of lamps in back passages was suspended, and kerbs had to be painted to facilitate movement in the darkness. Throughout the war period cases were brought before the Magistrate for failing to comply with blackout regulations, 340 cases for example during 1940. The following May no less an offender than the Council itself was admonished when the ornamental lamps of the Town Hall were left on, the unfortunate Janitor involved being fined £1 for the offence. Provision for the personal safety of the public took on a new urgency with the invasion of France. It was estimated that 60,000 people remained in Bootle after the outbreak of hostilities and would need to be provided with air raid shelter accommodation - both private shelters, and public shelters for those caught away from home during a raid. Anderson shelters were sunk into gardens, though these were uncommon in Bootle; surface shelters were built at the side of roads; basements were reinforced in houses and in business premises; and trench shelters were constructed in the three Bootle main parks. Later indoor steel shelters became available. In January 1940, the swings and see-saw were removed from Peel Road Playground to facilitate access to the large public air raid shelter.

Memories of time spent in air raid shelters remain - fear, boredom and discomfort are the three overriding features of contemporary accounts - fear particularly as people sat listening to the drone of the engines of enemy aircraft overhead, and to a "stick" of subsequent explosions coming closer. At the time there was much criticism levied at the condition of air raid shelters. Public shelters in particular were cold, very damp, badly ventilated, dimly lit, and provided crowded and often verminous accommodation. The shelter building programme had not been completed by the time air raids began and a number of those which had been built had to be demolished and rebuilt following inspection by the Senior Regional Technical Adviser.

Some public shelters became notorious for disorder - some of it sexual. Problems of vandalism led the Council to instigate a scheme of locking the shelters, the keys being left with a "responsible" resident. Some unfortunate choices of sound sleepers as "responsible" residents led to varying degrees of panic when the keyholder failed to be roused in the night by the sound of the siren, leaving neighbours locked out of the shelter. Shelter marshalls were later formally appointed in an attempt to scupper incidents of unruly behaviour, vandalism and too close a proximity to the opposite sex. Rules regulating conduct in shelters were eventually set out and displayed in public air raid shelters but often to little avail.

Twelve rest centres, for those made homeless following an attack, were established primarily in church halls. In all, over 7,000 people were to be provided with emergency shelter during the war and far greater numbers were sheltered by neighbours, relatives and friends.

The First Attacks

At 4.30 pm on 31 August 1939, the Emergency Committee, consisting of the Mayor, Nicholas Cullen, Simon Mahon, James Spence, Edwin Smith, A F Campbell and Harold Partington, the Town Clerk and ARP Controller, took control of all matters relating to the Civil Defence of the Borough, following issue of the formal instruction from H M Government. In the first two days of September the Education Department oversaw the evacuation of over 6,000 children of school age (and their teachers), along with 4,000 under-5s and almost 3,000 mothers - this was an incredible exercise involving precision planning and efficient organisation. The main destination was Southport. The following three days saw a significant number of children walking back to Bootle and the Emergency Committee continued to make evacuation plans for severe air raids to little avail. Parents soon joined their children in frustrating official arrangements. Out of 19,000 forms issued to parents requesting registration of potential evacuees, only 2,795 had been returned by April 1940, and 1,919 of those were from parents stating that they did not want their children evacuated at all! Contemporary accounts and reminiscences 50 years on are in complete accord - children would rather face the bombs than separation from family and home. By May 1940 the Emergency Committee had to apply to the Ministry of Home Security to re-open schools because of the vast numbers of returned evacuees roaming the streets with no education facilities available. (The teachers were still evacuated.)

The first attack of the war on Bootle took place at 10.22 pm on the night of 29 August 1940, and intermittent "clusters" of raids followed for months afterwards. At first raids consisted mainly of incendiary bombs causing fires, which were generally dealt with by local Fire Guards. High explosive bombs, which were more lethal, were also dropped. Exploding after penetrating the ground, these bombs tended to cause far more extensive damage, directly blasting buildings within the area of the explosion, and demolishing or damaging those close by.

December 1940: 23 Breeze Hill. A typical example of war damage. The back of the house was destroyed, the front showed no sign of damage and the attic windows remained unbroken. *(Sefton Libraries)*

September 1940:
The classic effect of a direct hit with an HE bomb.
(National Museums and Galleries on Merseyside)

It was on the night of the third air raid, on 31 August 1940, that Bootle experienced massive attack. Both high explosive bombs and incendiaries rained down, resulting in the first deaths and injuries of the war. A voluntary "trickle" evacuation or re-evacuation began to take place after these raids.

Attacks continued throughout September and not until the end of the month were nights free of either raids or sirens or false alarms. In mid-October the raids continued and only six days in November were free from alerts. Much of the destruction that occurred was fire damage to the timber yards and warehouses that lined the dock area, and to bridges, railway sidings and yards, although a number of houses were also destroyed or damaged. The fires from incendiary bombs lit the way for the German planes to pick out their targets for the high explosive bombs. The Dock area was too vast for the Dock authority to provide adequate emergency fire care. It was not until 12 March 1941 that the Cabinet decided, after prompting by the Bootle Council, to engage troops to begin fire watching at the Dockside until other arrangements could be made. The warehouse keepers acted as local guides for the troops.

From the end of November 1940 parachute mines began to fall on Bootle. These bombs exploded on impact with the surface rather than sinking into the ground and contained more explosive than the already familiar and lethal high explosives. The parachute mines caused damage over a vast area.

Early December was free from attack, but not from alerts, and from 20 December 1940, for three consecutive nights, Bootle and the surrounding areas received sustained bombardment. Raids began at tea time and lasted until the following morning. In 21 previous raids, the Borough had received something

Women examine the damage caused by an incendiary bomb on the Peter Marsh factory in Canal Street. *(Sefton Libraries)*

September 1940: A cotton warehouse on the corner of Nelson Street and Byng Street suffered severe damage. The half burnt cotton bales are still visible. *(Sefton Libraries)*

like 200 bombs. During these three nights of December it received an estimated third of that number again. The severity of the raids, which lasted an average of 10 1/2 hours, can be shown by the resultant destruction. 182 houses were destroyed by bombs and 1,600 were so damaged that the families had to be evacuated.

108 people lost their lives - including 26 children. 300 were injured and treated in hospital or at the first aid posts. Until that time the figures for dead and injured had stood at 44 and 242 respectively. The overall high proportion of child casualties was a result of the unofficial return home of evacuated children.

November 1940:
A child at the window of the flat above the newsagents in Peel Road, stares out in disbelief. "Scotts" still functioned but the other shops were temporarily abandoned.
(National Museums and Galleries on Merseyside)

Between this dreadful series of attacks and April 1941 there were only five attacks (plus 51 alerts). As many of the alerts came during the day, the nights were relatively peaceful and uninterrupted.

The May Blitz

Between 2nd and 8th May 1941 Bootle received something akin to saturation bombing, as a concentrated and prolonged assault was focussed on the Borough, and on the rest of Merseyside. It was described by German news bulletins as "... the heaviest raid yet delivered on an English town", locally it is still known as the "May Blitz". The December bombardment had been a mild precursor of what was to follow. The precautions of Major Salt were of little avail under such conditions: the scale of the attack was such that all public and emergency services collapsed and there was a complete breakdown of all normal life for a number of days. The mystery is that there was no major breakdown of public order at the same time.

The scale of destruction is hard to visualise. By 8 May almost 70% of the built-up area of Bootle was damaged, after seven nights of bombing. There were 191 major bomb blasts and uncountable numbers of minor devices, including incendiaries. Contemporary accounts reveal a dazed population emerging from shelters to find whole streets obliterated, rubble and sticks of furniture where homes once stood; craters in the roads; dense smoke and fires still burning.

And yet how is it, one woman remarked, that every window in the house was blown out, yet the six eggs on the shelf weren't even cracked?

Apocryphal perhaps, but women could still be seen blacking the steps of their near wrecked homes after the nightly onslaughts - a semblance of normality in the midst of chaos.

By the end of the week Bootle was without mains water, electricity and gas supplies, with 11 of its main sewers damaged and sewage seeping

Rescue work underway following a night of heavy bombing. ((National Museums and Galleries on Merseyside)

into the streets. Mobile water tanks were established throughout the Borough, replenished at intervals from outside supplies - including the provision at the ARP Headquarters. All the main roads were blocked by craters or rubble or burst water and sewerage pipes. No railway or tramway transport was operative and virtually all of the bridges were impassable. One third of the town's retail shops were demolished and nearly 100 of its factories, churches and schools, 33 of its public buildings were either badly damaged or obliterated. The GPO building in Balliol Road, Williams Toffee Factory, Scotts Bakery, one of the two main suppliers of bread in the Borough, Johnson's Dye Works, St Monica's Church, Vernons Pools, Orrell School, Mersey Cable Works, the Boy's Secondary School, St James' Senior Girls' School, the Branch Library, Marsh Lane Methodist Church - the list seems endless. The town's supply of anti-gas equipment and gas masks was destroyed as the ARP Headquarters was also struck.

Southey Street: The famous picture of the Bootle Blitz. The house was destroyed but the piano was blown into the street untouched and allegedly still playable.
(Sefton Libraries)

The May Blitz 1941: Johnsons Dyers and Cleaners, Linacre Road, virtually destroyed by incendiary bombs. Next day people still arrived for work. *(Sefton Libraries)*

The May Blitz 1941: Marsh Lane Station. The Railway line was missed but the station was wrecked. Note the war propaganda poster "Speed the ships" along with the more familiar Mackeson and Persil advertisements. *(Sefton Libraries)*

There was a desperate attempt to turn the air raid shelters from a temporary refuge to semi-permanent accommodation as the heavy bombing continued, and arrangements were made for bunks to be installed, the chemical toilets to be properly disposed of, the illegal sale of food countered, and for the rats to be dealt with - they too had sought refuge from the bombs. Vast numbers of residents left the town in what became a nightly exodus of vehicles and people to sleep overnight in the safety of outlying fields, returning the following morning. Maghull had made arrangements to take 1,750 refugees. One evening there were 6,000 and every church and school and hall was overflowing.

Law and order was more or less preserved until the bombing of the Knowsley Arms on Derby Road - news spread by word of mouth and crowds invaded the defenceless pub, consuming or removing the entire stock of wines, beers and spirits. The police found the crowd too hostile to make any more than a few token arrests. One man, hauled before the local magistrate, pleaded that he had only taken two sips of Walker's beer, which he didn't like anyway! Those who were caught vandalising property were dealt with by the local Magistrates.

Indeed juveniles accounted for the vast majority of cases of offences against property in the early part of the war. Even by 1940 the number of convictions against juveniles had more than doubled from the previous year, despite the fact that hundreds of children had been evacuated (even if only briefly) - 25% of the offenders being under the age of 12 years.

Fifty years on the reminiscences of those involved tend to dwell on the trivial and the inconsequential. Perhaps the nature of the horror makes it simply too painful to remember. For children the mountainous debris and rubble provided an exciting adventure playground. A part-demolished and abandoned haberdashers provided hours of fun - just opening drawers to find a shining button, or a colourful ribbon - goods were scarce. Secret dens could be built out of rubble and there was a never-ending supply of bricks to throw at those few windows which remained intact in near obliterated streets. Children unaware of the dangers of their playground foraged for wonderful treasure - precious pieces of shining shrapnel. Indeed swarms of children could be found digging in the rubble of a local sweet shop the day after it was demolished - toffee was a luxury none of them were going to let pass.

The May Blitz 1941:
65-67 Salisbury Road were hit by a land mine. Not even the air raid shelter (centre - white structure) survived intact.
(Sefton Libraries)

Several people were killed and injured when the entrance to the basement shelter beneath the shops in Stanley Road was hit by a high explosive bomb, causing the wall to collapse. St Andrew's Church Hall, one of the designated Rest Centres, had been accommodating 56 people made homeless from the previous night's raid. The Centre, staffed by volunteers of the WVS preparing breakfasts, also received a direct hit from a high explosive bomb - 37 people died. After these incidents attempts were made to make both homeless and voluntary helpers remain in shelters until the "all clear" was sounded. On the night of 7 May, there was a particularly gruesome incident. The temporary mortuary, established at Marsh Lane Baths, held 180 corpses from raids earlier in the week, all were awaiting burial, and 40 had yet to be identified. The mortuary received a direct hit and was razed to the ground. The remains were buried in a communal grave.

One Bootle myth of the war still holds that after the bombing of the Stanley Road shops, the shelter was simply levelled to the ground with the bodies still in it as "they" could not be bothered to dig the corpses out. The truth is almost as dreadful. The bodies were dug out and taken to the temporary mortuary but the Baths were razed to the ground by fire before identification could take place.

(far left)
The May Blitz 1941:
Destruction of classroom number 4 in the Bedford Road Infants School which was hit by incendiary bombs. The clock - showing the same time - 11.34 pm still survives.
(Sefton Libraries)

(below)
The May Blitz 1941:
The junction of Stanley Road and Little Strand Road. Many people lost their lives while sheltering in the shop cellars.
(Sefton Libraries)

The May Blitz 1941:
The picture shows what was left of St. Andrew's Church Hall, Linacre Road, following a direct hit by an HE bomb.
(Sefton Libraries)

Other incidents illustrate the reality of coping in dire circumstances, and the quirks of "fate" which lent hope sometimes tinged with farce to the most impossible of situations. One such incident is described in a report on conditions in the Bootle General Hospital on the night of 7 May by James Moroney, who had been transferred from Ormskirk Emergency Hospital just two days previously. In the first hour of the raid on 7 May, casualties were brought in at a rate of one per minute - an impossible situation to cope with. At the end of this hour the hospital was damaged and the wards were in chaos - three bombs had landed close by. Some patients were in bed, some on stretchers under the beds. The thin fabric of the huts, used as temporary wards, and glass from the windows were scattered over everything. As the blackout material had been blown away, torches could not be used. Meanwhile, ambulances continued to arrive and no communication with the Control Centre was possible as telephone lines were down. The dead were laid on the lawns and the injured given what shelter the damaged hospital could afford. About 3.00 am, a fleet of ambulances arrived and all the patients were evacuated by 5.00 am. Mr Moroney commented on the "impossibility" of giving proper service to casualties in a building which lay within the target area. It afforded no protection either for staff or patients and the only result of designating it the casualty reception centre was negative - numbers of people gathering at one spot where the probability of further injury was high, where crowds of friends and relatives collected and where the staff were rendered helpless by the scale of the damage. Mr Moroney felt that the immediate transfer to Ormskirk, ten miles away, was the "proper" solution to the Bootle problem.

Mr A L Cooper, Superintendant of the Bootle General Hospital, later gave his impressions of the occurrences on the night of 7 - 8 May.

> "One of the many incidents of the May 1941 raids on Merseyside was the damaging of the Bootle General Hospital and its subsequent evacuation at the height of a prolonged raid. It is said that troubles never come singly, and this proved true as far as the hospital was concerned on the night of May 7 - 8. Up to then we had escaped with only minor damage but within one half hour we had scores of incendiary bombs, a direct hit on the first aid post, a delayed action HE, only twenty yards from where raid casualties were being received, and finally two landmines fell near the boundary wall and finished the job. A hasty tour of the hospital revealed that there were only three casualties from these incidents, but the wards were clearly unusable. A remarkable calmness among both patients and staff. The system whereby patients were placed on one mattress underneath their beds, while a second mattress remained on the wire springs of the bed to afford protection, undoubtedly saved many from injury. The staff were told to wrap patients in blankets and prepare for evacuation.
>
> The next problem was to establish contact with the Control Centre for assistance. Electrical, gas and telephone services had long been interrupted but with that hope which springs eternal in every breast a visit was made to the telephone room.
>
> The light of the moon, its coldness now enriched with the glow of many fires, revealed the operator still sitting patiently in front of her "dead" switchboard, windows gone and debris all around. A thoughtful operator at the exchange inquired if the hospital had any messages.
>
> Contact was made with the Control and transport requested for evacuation. Before the conversation could be completed the board again became "dead". For a second time fortune favoured us, as on leaving the telephone room, there unmistakably was a solitary bus coming along the road. This stopped in response to signals and once again the kindness and helpful spirit which seemed to prevail on these occasions was in evidence, as the driver immediately agreed to take a bus load of patients to the nearest hospitals. Sitting cases from the wards were transferred to the bus. Further transport soon began to arrive in response to the SOS and before the raid was over, all patients had been evacuated and without a further single casualty. Within six weeks the damage to the hospital was repaired and once again we were ready for any eventuality.
>
> The main impressions left were the magnificent behaviour of both patients and staff. The greatest ordeal was the waiting period for casualties to arrive, but once there was something to do all feelings of fear disappeared and everyone worked regardless of personal danger. We found that the deadliest thing was not the bomb, but continued lack of sleep. Four and five nights and days of receiving, treating and transferring casualties, yes, but when it came to the sixth and seventh nights, we felt only a few more would bring work to a standstill.
>
> There was a great deal of humour too, even from the old lady of 70 years who, although a casualty, and in spite of being lucky to have just escaped with her life, insisted that her son went back to find her false teeth as she was 'ashamed to appear before company looking like an old hag'."

In all 102 men, 80 women and 40 children lost their lives during those seven nights, and a further 35 bodies were unidentifiable. A total of 257 lives lost. Of 261 seriously injured people treated at the hospital, primarily for scalp wounds and fractures, two thirds were operated upon. A further 481 people received less serious injuries. Five were reported missing believed killed.

An astonishing 75% of houses in Bootle were either destroyed or wrecked during this one week. A black humour soon emerged. The level of damage to a person's home became the subject of perverse pride. Those with houses untouched or only slightly damaged were deemed not to have done their duty in the battle.

The May Blitz 1941: 120-136 Benedict Street were severely damaged but the windows of the house adjacent largely remained untouched. The sticky tape fixed to windows to reduce blast was made notorious by "Lord Haw Haw" who sent a special radio message to the people of Bootle to tell them that "the kisses on the windows" would not save them. Note the picture still hanging on the wall. *(Sefton Libraries)*

The Aftermath

No less than 20,000 people were made homeless following the May raids, and with 11 of the 12 rest centres out of operation urgent action was required for re-housing. Arrangements had already been made for almost 5,000 billets, in addition to the evacuation scheme and voluntary dispersal. On the morning of 3 May, three quarters of that accommodation itself had been damaged. Hasty arrangements were made via the Regional Organiser to find places outside the town for the thousands made homeless. Between 7.00 pm and 10.30 pm, approximately 10,000 people, having congregated in school halls, were removed outside the immediate area of danger on foot and by every conceivable means of transport - many to nearby towns of Huyton, Waterloo, Crosby, Formby and Maghull.

The May Blitz 1941: Junction of Litherland Road and Marsh Lane. The houses were completely obliterated. Stunned residents survey the damage. *(Sefton Libraries)*

The military authorities provided 300 men to help the Borough Engineers Department clear away the mountains of street debris, until arrangements were made for assistance from outside contractors. Emergency repairs were initially carried out to houses until the full extent of the necessary restoration situation could be determined. St John's School was turned into a secure storage area for those personal belongings which had survived.

The problem of feeding those who remained, given the deficiencies in the food supply, were partly overcome with the aid of the mobile canteens, and through "British Restaurants", as well as by help from outside. Retail shops deemed to be selling essential goods, but which had been damaged during the week, were issued with small collapsible booths by the Ministry of Supply.

The May Blitz:
Rimrose Road experienced severe bombing. These two pictures show Council workmen (centre) and troops (left) in salvage rescue work. The car FBB 456 has only one "blackout" headlight, one is missing.
(National Museums and Galleries on Merseyside)

Twenty five mobile canteens were sent from around the region to add to the five owned by the Borough to help feed the homeless. One ton of corned beef was used on the first day for sandwiches, an average of 39,000 portions of sandwiches, tea/soup or cocoa were prepared each day. At first the British Restaurants were established in large marquees in the parks, until accommodation was secured on the Dock Road, the Welsh Chapel in Peel Road and at the Presbyterian Church Hall in Hawthorne Road. The first British Restaurant opened on the Sunday, staffed through the labour exchange and furnished by the Government. By the Tuesday all were open, serving approximately 10,000 meals per day - free on the first day and for a small charge thereafter: breakfast for 5d, dinner for 8d. By the end of the war the Restaurants - the "Mersey", "Victoria" and "Derby" - were still serving some 22,000 dinners per month.

The Salvation Army Building, Stanley Road, suffered structural damage during a raid in September 1940. "HITLER - THE BEAST OF BERLIN" continued to draw large audiences at the "Palladium" - air raids permitting.
(Sefton Libraries)

Aid of various kinds was brought to Bootle from across the North West region and from as far afield as Hull and Stoke-on-Trent. The aid was desperately needed and gratefully received with the exception of para-typhoid fever which originated from an out-of-town bakery supplying bread and cakes: the disease affected 59 people between June and August 1941. Later the British War Relief Society of the United States donated £600 for relief of air raid distress with the express wish for it to benefit the children of Bootle. A committee set up to allocate the money decided that prams were at a premium, hence a number were purchased and issued to local mothers on a "buy back" scheme.

Four and a half months followed free from attack. On 20 October 1941 Bootle received its final onslaught from the Luftwaffe. Casualties were heavier than would have been expected that night as many people had not sheltered immediately and had waited for the sound of the first far-away bombs to drop. Two bombs fell close together near Surrey Street, they were the first of the night and created the largest single incident of the war - 109 casualties.

In all, Bootle experienced 502 air raid alerts, the final one on 29 December 1942. 85% of its buildings were damaged, and 1,886 civilians were killed or injured. This small independent Borough, hardly mentioned in the chronicles of the Second World War, suffered by far the highest proportion of deaths per 1,000 of population on Merseyside. It is very difficult to compare like with like in any examination of the statistics of death by enemy action, but it would appear that Bootle suffered more than any other town in the United Kingdom.

The danger faced by the civil defence personnel is shown in the number of awards received - 2 OBEs, 3 MBEs, 17 BEMs, 6 George Medals, 1 King's Police Medal, and 16 Commendations.

Sex, Drink, Vermin and Other Minor Consequences

In addition to its bombardment from on high, there were other dangers for the people in Bootle. The rat population flourished in the war and certainly became more visible as the bombing disturbed its normal abodes. An all-out war was raged against rats and two men were employed as rat-catchers during the mid-war period, as part of a National Infestation Order. The Medical Officer of Health estimated that 12,921 sewer rats were destroyed (one wonders at the precision of this "estimate") - ".. and although only 169 bodies were recovered, independent observers reported large numbers washed out of the main sewer outfall by the Gladstone Dock".

Rationing meant few luxuries: a flourishing "Black Market": and cases of forgery of ration books. Some shopkeepers were believed to have profited well from the "select" goods kept under the counter for "select" customers. Indeed a significant number of prosecutions were brought for, amongst other things, selling cheese, meat and vegetables over the recommended price; watering down of milk; and for using faulty scales. For many, fruits, sweets and even basic necessities could sometimes be enjoyed when the ships docked and fathers, brothers and uncles, returning home from the convoys, or helping to unload the cargo, would bring home the miniscule "perks" of their jobs. Onions, sugar, butter, fruit - the bounty would be shared amongst many, families and neighbours - or sold.

Offences involving "intoxicating liquor" - either its illegal sale or consumption after hours increased during the period, while those for betting and gaming declined. Thefts from gas and electricity meters in unsecured houses, as the occupants were sheltering during raids, certainly increased.

Attempted suicides decreased - the Chief Constable reporting that the figures for 1940 were the "... lowest for a considerable number of years" - perhaps war provided a new interest in life.

Bootle suffered inevitably during the war from afflictions of a more traditional kind. The incidence of new cases of venereal disease more than doubled during the war period. Dr Wood, stating the obvious that the figures "... indicate freer indulgence in promiscuous sexual intercourse", dispatched Officers to visit persistent non-attenders at treatment clinics in an effort to combat locally what was a growing national problem.`

A virtual trebling of the number of illegitimate births posed problems. By January 1944, single mothers were offered help and advice from Council health visitors in the moral and practical welfare of themselves and their children. The local newspaper of the time had little doubt where the blame lay claiming that young girls, catching the tram to Seaforth and "applying cosmetics in public" were luring young sailors into "immorality and drunkenness". The reminiscences of the Merchant Navy and Royal Navy men 50 years on suggest that the sailors offered little resistance.

Marriage too increased in popularity. In 1940 there had been 891 marriages in the town, compared with 731 the previous year and 653 in 1938. Perhaps it was in part due to the Civil Registrar's new power "... to reduce at his discretion in necessitous cases, the total fee in respect of marriage of a member of Forces below commissioned rank, to the amount of 10s". Perhaps also the closer proximity of sudden death concentrated minds on personal relationships of either a fleeting or permanent nature.

Prospect of Peace : Reconstruction

By 1942, with months free from attack, the town began to look to the future and a Reconstruction Committee was set up to deal with post-war unemployment, the care of disabled citizens and industrial and economic development. It was estimated that over 900 houses were needed just to rehouse Bootle people billeted outside the Borough. This was in addition to the acute housing shortage already mentioned that existed before 1939. The Medical Officer of Health suggested that over 7,000 houses would have to be built in total in the post-war redevelopment. The acquisition of houses for flats, planning for new housing and erection of temporary homes were priorities as the threat of further attack receded. Land in outlying areas was eventually purchased or requisitioned for what was to be a major post-war house building programme.

The last two years of the war saw attention focussed on more routine matters of civic organisation - dealing with fires and bomb sites and also with vandalism to the now disused air raid shelters, many of which had been blocked up by the

October 1941: Bewildered residents survey the damaged caused by two HE bombs falling together in Surrey Street. It was the largest single incident of the war in Bootle. *(Sefton Libraries)*

end of 1944. There were the dangers to children caused by derelict property and particular attention was paid to the problem after a number of deaths by drowning because of damage to the Canal walls. Thefts from civil defence properties were becoming a public scandal as a section of the population saw Government property as fair game. On one occasion even an ambulance was stolen. By Christmas 1944 it was considered safe for three National Fire Service stations to close, the numbers of personnel in the Civil Defence services were drastically reduced and the services themselves were gradually wound down. Blast protection walls were removed from Corporation premises.

The May Blitz 1941:
Soldiers having a smoke during rescue work in Southey Street. The houses on both sides of the road were hit.
(Sefton Libraries)

But the routine of the Home Front ground on. The Borough's Salvage Committee, which had operated throughout the war, continued in its scrap, paper and book salvage work. Their slogan "From Home Front to Second Front" was printed on the back of the 1943 Rates demand. They co-operated in the regular Lancashire Salvage Drives - "Salvage Saves Shipping" was the theme of the October event in the same year. A curious drive was that to collect gramophone records, in April 1945 the WVS collected 80 lbs of unbroken records and 35 lbs of broken ones, these could be sold at 22 shillings per hundredweight - exactly for what is now a mystery of war.

Provision was made for the annual "Holidays at Home" summer entertainments provided for those unable to get away from Bootle for a holiday. These were to include cricket matches and tennis tournaments, bowling competitions, swimming galas, sports days, band performances, children's talent contests, and dancing in the Derby and North Parks. In 1944 Marsh Lane Baths were reopened to provide swimming facilities.

By November 1944 a "Preparations for Peace" Committee was in existence. The VE day celebrations six months later were lavish, requiring unaccustomed street lighting in Oriel, Merton, Trinity, Balliol and part of Stanley Roads, with floodlighting of the Town Hall, and high powered electric lamps "... to light up as large a portion of Derby Park as possible, where dance orchestras were to play; two orchestras at the Town Hall; community singing at the Town Hall to be broadcast to the surrounding streets; flags, bunting and a procession".

Soldiers assisting in clear-up operation in number 264 Hawthorne Road. (Sefton Libraries)

After the burst of wild celebration at the end of the war, Bootle returned to grim reality and coping with a new surge of unemployment as the armed forces were demobilised. Reconstruction was hard and the rather desperate co- operative spirit of the war slowly faded. The flags, crests and battle honours of Bootle's adopted war ships - the *Starling,* the *Swift,* the *Bootle,* and the *Erne* and their like were hung with due ceremony in the Council chamber. They remain an intensely moving sight. It is poignant that there is no similar tribute to the merchant seamen from Bootle and those who adopted Bootle as their second home. Nor is there a fitting memorial to the ordinary people of Bootle who lived, worked, suffered and died from 1939 to 1945.

THE WAR AT SEA

The First Round At Sea

David Lowe's comic cartoon character Colonel Blimp earned a certain notoriety during the 30s. Whatever the evidence for smugness and lack of preparation in the Army, there is little doubt that Colonel Blimp would have felt remarkably comfortable in the higher reaches of the Admiralty. The British Navy had failed to see the real significance of the U-boat campaign between 1916 and 1918. In the First World War the British Navy resisted almost to the point of defeat the telling statistical arguments for the convoy system. The Admiralty spent most of the war looking for a great naval battle - a second Trafalgar: a fleet campaign when the clear and overwhelming might of the capital ships, the battleships and the heavy cruisers, could be brought to bear upon the German Navy. The Royal Navy was obsessed with controlling the seas but in controlling the surface of the seas it had signally failed by 1916 to defend the merchantmen from underwater peril. The principle of convoy was the principle of defence, not of attack, and defence did not accord with overwhelming naval might. Only the threat of defeat brought the Admiralty, reluctantly, grudgingly, to the view that convoy alone would avert strangulation.

Against these convoys was pitched the submarine, a vessel with its own curious history. Bizarrely, it was developed in 1870 by an American Irish Fenian for the express purpose of terrorist attacks upon the British Empire. In the 40 years before the First World War all the major maritime powers expressed interest in John Philip Holland's design. Its full potential, however, was not realised until well into the Great War. By February 1917 Germany estimated that if they managed to sink around 600,000 tons a month of merchant shipping plying the supply routes to Great Britain and France, Great Britain might be taken out of the war.

Initially the Germans achieved their targets to the extent that their Chief of naval staff estimated that British trade could be strangled within five months. At the insistence of Lloyd George the British replied with the convoy system, accompanied by primitive listening devices on warships and by the development of depth charges, but despite those protective measures by the end of the War a quarter of the world's tonnage may still have been lost to the German U-boats - nearly 6,000 ships. This is an amazing total in the context of only two years of unrestricted submarine warfare. Yet convoys worked, Britain survived, and, most tellingly, survived long enough for American intervention and supplies to be brought by convoys to the European war.

Between the Wars

The lessons of the Great War were not properly learned by either side. Despite the success of the convoy system, traditional naval policy soon reasserted itself

The Nelsonian hold based upon the 19th century concept of the ship of the line and its Dreadnought successors was still too strong, the concept of aggressive warfare and an instinctive contempt for defensive tactics too ingrained. As a result there was little preparation in the 1930s for defensive convoy tactics. There was no overall strategy at the start of the war and the ablest officers in anti-submarine warfare were not in a position to influence policies. It was not only that the higher reaches of the Admiralty were in the hands of "the bloody gunnery officers obsessed with the calibre inches of their guns" (as a contemporary naval officer remarked) but that those same officers had a misplaced faith in technological development which led them to believe that the submarine threat had been beaten for all time.

The Anti-Submarine Detection Investigation Committee of 1917 had given its acronym "ASDIC" to the "underwater eye". ASDIC is described in more detail later: suffice to say that training demonstrations for Winston Churchill (then an MP) in Weymouth Bay bore no relation to later convoy escort strategies against U-boat "wolf pack" tactics. A memorandum of 1936 stated with breathtaking smugness that "... so important is the development of ASDIC that the submarine should never again be able to present us with the problem we were faced with in 1917". It was not until 1937 that there was any significant attempt to consider an escort strategy. Belatedly a stand-in escort was developed from a commercial whale-catcher design and this became the naval class corvette. Sturdy and incredibly uncomfortable, slow (16 knots) and designed for coastal work, this ugly, improbable and inappropriately named "flower" class vessel became the standard convoy escort. The first corvette became a naval joke before distinguishing itself in the bloodiest convoy battle of the war, HX229/SC122:

Destroyer (by signal flag)	"What are you?"
Corvette	"Periwinkle."
Destroyer	"Can I stick a pin in you?"
Corvette	"No, I am a pale blue flower not a shellfish."
Destroyer	"Then I will come over and fertilise you."

A Flower Class Corvette in the Mersey. *(Imperial War Museum)*

The Germans were similarly ill-prepared in 1939, their Naval preparations were limited in scope, not by virtue of the 1919 Treaty of Versailles which had placed the most severe restrictions on naval building but by confusion over military aims. In fact the restrictive provisions on German rearmament were ignored during the 1930s in an increasingly blatant fashion and submarine development had gone on to the extent that its technical superiority was unsurpassed. What was missing was a grasp of strategy, not by the Navy itself, but by the Nazi leadership. In the mid-thirties Admiral Karl Doenitz had emerged as the supreme U-boat theoretical tactician and he became eventual Commander of the U-boat fleet. However, at the start of the war his submarine headquarters in Heligoland had only 39 U-boats for operation outside the Baltic. Doenitz calculated, probably correctly, that with 300 U-boats he could have forced the British Isles to seek terms with Germany. If Adolf Hitler, as supreme commander of German forces, did have an overriding strategy, he expected a short campaign in continental Europe, with enough pressure upon Britain to lead to a negotiated settlement in Germany's favour. Initially he had little understanding or interest in possible naval campaigns. Hitler, if the evidence of "Mein Kampf" is anything to go by, had always looked to German expansion to the east, with Russia as the inevitable enemy. Both the aborted invasion of Britain in 1940/41 and his conversion to massive submarine warfare in the Atlantic Approaches were a typical Hitlerian response to "providence".

U-boat = Unterseeboot = under sea boat.

The Battle for the Supply Lines

As in the First World War, when military attention turned inevitably to the lines of supply, both sides struggled to make good their deficiencies, Germany to produce the submarines to starve Britain to submission, Britain to combat the threat. The real battle for Britain took place in the Western Approaches and in the home ports. The initial advantage lay with Germany and with Admiral Doenitz, a commanding officer who was technically brilliant and an effective, if personally distant, leader of men. Perhaps most significantly Doenitz was a professional officer who never incurred the distrust of Hitler, the ex-First World War corporal turned Fuhrer who retained an instinctive contempt for the officer caste.

Germany's development of U-boat tactics in the 1930s was radical and brilliant particularly since as a U-boat captain, Doenitz himself, while brave, had not been particularly impressive. Doenitz applied torpedo boat strategy to submarine warfare. He developed the concept of "pack" tactics using large numbers of U-boats to attack on the surface at night. He planned to use his boats at key locations in the Atlantic in such a way as to create a loosely- linked net across the significant trade routes. The theory was based on a careful calculation of the strengths and weaknesses of the advanced German U- boat design, and of the likely opposition. In particular, the submarines on the surface were capable of up to 20 knots but only one third of that underwater. He also recognised that the capacity to submerge was more useful as a means of secret approach and retreat rather than long distance travel and that the torpedo was a very effective weapon against any type of ship.

Doenitz had also absorbed the statistical lessons of 1916 - 1918. It had been calculated that Britain required between 50 and 60 million tons of goods annually. The bulk of this trade was carried in approximately 3,000 British merchant ships. Doenitz's calculation that he needed 300 U-boats was based on simple statistical analysis. If the First World War targets of about 3 sinkings per month per U-boat were achieved and if one sixth of U-boats were on patrol duty in any one month, then half the available British ships might be destroyed in a year.

On the opening day of the War, U-boat U30 sank a civilian liner, the *Athenia*, to international outrage and against Hitler's express orders. The outrage in Britain was such that the *Times* warned against the ill treatment of Dachsunds which were "... being singled out continually as being symbolically teutonic". More conventionally within the "rules" of war, a courageous submarine attack on the British Home Fleet in the main Scapa Flow anchorage, off northern Scotland, had caused pandemonium and humiliation with the loss of a battleship The *Royal Oak*. Within the first week of war 80,000 tons of shipping had been sunk and by November 1939 Churchill was describing U-boats as the "acme of villainy". By Christmas, British supply lines were in chaos: at a time when General Ironside in France was loudly proclaiming that "Hilter had missed the bus", the Cabinet was being told that half a million tons of shipping had been lost to submarines, mines and surface raiders, that there was only three weeks supply of wheat left and two weeks supply of iron ore. After a bad start, the new year brought some relief. Initially the arming of some merchant vessels provided the pretext for unrestricted submarine warfare and in February 1940 250,000 tons of shipping were lost to 10 operational U- boats. However, U-boats were diverted to support the German invasion of Norway and a more effective organisation of the convoy system started to take effect. By May 1940 when the Germans opened the Western offensive against France, detailed statistical analysis in Western Approaches command was showing that escorted convoys were reducing the "kill" rate.

The transfer of shipwrecked merchant sailors from one ship to another.
(Imperial War Museum)

The Campaign from the Brittany Ports

It was the fall of France and the opening of France's Atlantic ports in June 1940 to the U-boats which changed the whole nature of the submarine campaign. In four months in the summer of 1940, 274 ships were believed to have been sunk by Doenitz's crews. At this stage it dawned upon Hitler that the submarine command's dream of the total destruction of Britain's merchant fleet was a real possibility. The statistics are stunning. By January 1941 annual imports to the United Kingdom had decreased from more than 50 million tons to about 35 million tons. Only three months later, it was calculated that, on an annual basis, another 5 million tons had been lost, with food imports estimated to be down to the minimum subsistence level of about 15 million tons. In June 1941 alone, a

1945: Picture shows the operations room at Derby House, Liverpool. Here a Wren is at work on the enemy submarine reports board. The report is an imaginary one used in the film being "shot" by the Army Film Unit cameramen at the Headquarters of Western Approaches.
(Imperial War Museum)

dozen operational U-boats sank over 300,000 tons of shipping. The key was Doenitz's control of the French Atlantic ports and the development of huge submarine pens, particularly at Lorient in Brittany. After Lorient, other bases at Brest, St Nazaire, La Rochelle and as far south as Bordeaux were developed.

Not only were the Western Approaches threatened but shipping routes to the Mediterranean and the South Atlantic were also within submarine operational range. Doenitz operated the Atlantic campaign from a chateau at Kerneval, near the main Lorient base. He worked closely with a small team of ex-submarine officers, an arrangement which reflected at the central headquarters the closely-bonded nature of the whole submarine service - a noteworthy feature of submarine warfare on both sides. His morning staff conferences directed the entire U-boat campaign. This arrangement was mirrored in underground headquarters in Derby House behind Liverpool Town Hall, where Admiral Noble, and later Admiral Horton, conducted, on Britain's behalf, a similar operation, at first defensive and then increasingly offensive, against the submarine threat.

September 1940: British children who had been rescued from a ship torpedoed by a U-boat on their way to Canada, now safely back at port. *(Imperial War Museum)*

The War of Attrition

The next two years saw a complex naval campaign with German submarines in the ascendent until May 1943. The crisis of summer 1941 forced the British to push the Atlantic convoys as far north as weather and ice would allow. The inadequate naval capability for providing escorts was alleviated in part by Roosevelt's "sale" of 50 First World War vintage destroyers to the Royal Navy in exchange for long lease of British air bases. The great weakness in British naval defences was the inadequacy of air cover which left a significant area of mid Atlantic uncovered by allied aircraft - "the air gap". This allowed Doenitz's U-boats to act as surface torpedo boats at night and render ASDIC inoperational.

By the beginning of 1942 the British maritime fleet was down from 17 million tons to about 14 million tons despite massive new building. This was the U-boat's "happy" time. It seemed their captains could not fail. In January 1942, for example, 30 oil tankers were sunk leaving the Gulf of Mexico refineries to sail up the Eastern coast of America and in the first six months of the year, shipping lost on the United States Atlantic seaboard alone was well over 600,000 tons. Violent death at sea has always had its own peculiar horrors. The Second World War made commonplace newer variants. The unmitigated dreadfulness of a lingering death in a depth-charged submarine was, however, matched within the oil tanker fleet. Oil would insulate a man from exposure and drowning, from the "normal" deaths at sea, but if it did not burn him alive on the surface of the sea it would clog his lungs and slowly choke him.

(right)
A survivor from a U-boat being lifted onto the deck of *HMS Swansea.*
(Imperial War Museum)

Seamen being rescued after 15 days on board a raft. They had no food left and only 2 gallons of water. They used to flash tin lids in the sun to catch the attention of passing ships. *(Imperial War Museum)*

Slowly, the United States established their own convoys on the eastern seaboard and as their navy exerted pressure on the U-boats, Doenitz moved his submarine packs back into the mid Atlantic. He now had well over his target of 300 U-boats and rarely would operational strength fall below 50 on the Atlantic trade routes. Soon his crews were exceeding the 1941 sinkages and by the end of 1942 over 100 ships a month were being sunk. The "wolf pack" system was constantly being refined and Doenitz himself never relaxed his close personal control by radar from his chateau headquarters.

An acute sense of crisis on both sides pervaded the early months of 1943. By January the number of operational U-boats had risen to its highest point of the war with approximately 100 on patrol at any one time, at least enough theoretically to paralyse the British supply lines. But the Allies were making slow in-roads into the "kill ratio". What in 1941 and 1942 had been a fairly consistent ratio - one submarine lost for each 13 merchant ships - had now improved in favour of the Allies to one U-boat loss to approximately every 10 merchant ships sunk. It is also estimated that, by now, the Allies had 500 escorts at their disposal and Captain F J "Johnny" Walker, one of that band of despised inter-war anti-submarine experts, was about to receive the recognition he deserved with the formation of the free-ranging "hunting" support groups for separate attacks on U-boats. Simultaneously the Allies were within reach of the last few miles of the "air gap" in mid-Atlantic with aircraft operating from the UK base (in Northern Ireland), from St John's in Canada, and from Reykjavik in Iceland. On both sides radar data was providing high quality intelligence as to the location of convoys or wolf packs. By the spring of 1943 the outcome of the Battle of the Atlantic hung in the balance. The key to understanding the ultimate allied victory lay in the fate of two convoys numbered HX229 and SC122.

(top right)
The surrender of *U826*. German ratings throw their ammunition panniers into the sea watched by a British naval armed guard. *(Imperial War Museum)*

(right)
The surrender of *U10-09*. In the background is the Captain's class frigate *HMS Byron*, one of a successful escort group of U-boat hunters. *(Imperial War Museum)*

K508

The Turning Point

The fate of these convoys was, at the time, seen as a disaster for the Allies and for the Royal and Merchant Navies in particular. There is a curious and paradoxical parallel with Dunkirk. Dunkirk was a defeat celebrated as a victory. HX229 and SC122 were seen initially in March 1943 as a British disaster. In fact, they were the turning point of the whole Atlantic campaign albeit paid for with the lives of 372 merchant seamen and 22 ships, the highest single convoy loss of the war.

A British convoy moving up one of the seaways off the British Coast. *(Imperial War Museum)*

In February 1943 and the first week of March, 100 ships gathered in the Hudson River in Canada to form the basis of the two great convoys. SC122 was due to sail on 5 March and HX229 three days later. The routes planned for them were broadly similar, following a conventional convoy path north of the normal trade route from North America to the United Kingdom. SC122 was accompanied by 10 escorts, two of which were from the United States, while HX229 had 11 ships, of which one was American. Significantly there was no free-ranging support group such as Captain Walker's Second Support Group to provide additional protection and, of course, at this stage in the war, both convoys might still have to spend up to six days in the air gap in mid-Atlantic where no protection was available from land based aircraft. No escorts capable of launching aircraft at sea were available for either convoy. On the face of it convoy SC122 was the more vulnerable. It was termed a slow convoy with an estimated sailing speed of 6 or 7 knots as opposed to HX229 which could sail several knots faster. Moreover SC122 had older, slower ships carrying general freight, and several ships carried explosives. HX229, although faster, included a significant number of tankers carrying not only fuel oil but also much more volatile lubricants and aviation petrol.

The U-boat packs, by a combination of luck and planning, were at full strength as the convoy sailed out. As many as 14 U-boats in a pack named "Raubgraf" (Robber Baron) were only 750 miles off the Canadian coast, while two further packs totalling 31 boats were forming two lines in the middle of the Atlantic - a total of 42 U-boats, plus supply tanker U-boats.

The convoy escorts, then, were outnumbered by two to one and the U-boats were expecting them. There is some irony in the fact that they were expecting a totally different and much larger expedition, the HX229A, due to set out at a later date. HX229 met the fate that Doenitz's Headquarters had planned for HX229A, and SC122 was caught in close proximity.

Appalling weather conditions provided cover for the early progress of both convoys. SC122 missed the advance line of U-boats off Newfoundland altogether. The weather secured a similarly uneventful passage for HX229 (though the weather was ferocious enough to sink one of the escorts *HMS Campobello* in waves 40 feet high). Then HX229 was discovered purely by chance by a U-boat returning to base. Its single radio transmission was sufficient to cause Doenitz to bring the "Robber Baron" line from Newfoundland and part of the other two packs towards the convoy.

U-boat Headquarters were convinced that they had now discovered SC122 and not HX229 or HX229A. It was immaterial because the converging packs of U-boats were sailing on a collision course for both convoys. HX229 was attacked first. By 16 March the convoy was facing seven U-boats. A Norwegian grain and ore freighter *Elin K* was hit at 10.00 pm and quickly sank. An hour later, a Dutch frigate and American Liberty ship were hit. A contemporary account of the destruction of HX229 describes the calm, stoical fortitude of the Dutch and Norwegian crews in contrast with the panic of the men on the Liberty ship. By now, Commander Luther, the inexperienced commander of the HX229 escort group was in an impossible position, attempting to protect his remaining ships, hunt U-boats and rescue survivors simultaneously. At half past midnight a second Liberty ship carrying sugar rations sufficient for the entire British population was torpedoed and abandoned by its crew, perhaps prematurely, and was subsequently sunk by *HMS Volunteer*, one of the escorting destroyers. Two hours later two U-boats fired eight torpedoes, some of them of the particularly dangerous circling "FAT" variety and hit another American freighter. There was tense calm until 2.30 am when a single U-boat crept through the inadequate escort screen, despatched five torpedoes and hit three ships at random. A general cargo ship, a meat freighter and an oil tanker were lost.

As dawn broke, on 17 March, the U-boats retreated out of visual range of the escorts. Eight merchantmen had already been lost that night. The afternoon saw the U-boat packs reinforced by two further submarines and a Dutch and British freighter were hit by torpedoes at long range. By now, the escorts were loaded with survivors. Repeated and random depth-charging by the desperate escort captains gave HX229 a night without incident, but of considerable fear. The following morning - 18 March - was likewise artificially calm but at 1 o'clock one of the "Harrier" line of U-boats found a way through the escorts and destroyed another American Liberty ship, the *William Eustis* on its first voyage, carrying powdered milk, the staple food supplement for Britain's wartime infants. The sea frothed white with milk as the ship settled.

Meanwhile, a single U-boat, U338, under the impression that it was attacking HX229, was wreaking havoc on SC122. Some time after two in the morning on 17 March, this single U-boat sank a general cargo ship, a Dutch food oil freighter and two British general cargo ships. Although it is not the intention in this chapter to consider the human element of the war at sea the extraordinary bravery of a Dutch freighter captain stands out; in the middle of the night Captain van Os swam round his ship's lifeboats and then right around the Royal Navy corvette *Saxifrage* in order to satisfy himself that the rescuing corvette had not overlooked any of his sailors. He survived but despite his valiant attempts his crew were not so lucky - 18 of his men died in the cruel March sea. The partnership between the *Saxifrage* and Captain van Os was continued in the Mediterranean later that year when the unfortunate Dutchman was yet again rescued by this Flower class corvette as he experienced his second U-boat sinking.

British seamen being rescued by the US coastguards after many days on a life raft. *(Imperian War Museum)*

That afternoon of 17 March, U338 hit a Panamanian freighter loaded with military stores with four torpedoes and broke her in two, and, with its position now signalled, Doenitz ordered further support in the shape of six submarines from one of the three wolf packs to join it. By the evening, this support had arrived and a refrigerator ship and a freighter carrying iron filings were destroyed.

But by 18 March the convoys were within range of aircraft flying from Belfast, and U-boat activities were restricted. The engagement with both convoys petered to an end. The escort groups had been increased as a measure of desperation and no less than seven air squadrons were patrolling in relay in an attempt to keep U-boats at a distance and drive them below the surface. As many as 12 submarines had been circling the convoy: by 18 March that number was down by about a third.

The fate of HX229 and SC122 is dwelt upon deliberately. It was the largest sustained battle of the Atlantic war. More than 40 U-boats were deployed against nearly 100 merchant ships, some 20 Royal Navy destroyers and corvettes, and a couple of American coastguard cutters. Over 160,000 tons of supplies went down with the 22 merchant ships sunk. There is no doubt that the level of loss in this mid March battle - nearly 150,000 tons of shipping in what was, in effect, a single engagement, was a rate of destruction no shipping replacement programme could be expected to sustain. To match it, the British and American shipyards would have had to produce over 7,000,000 tons a year of shipping.

Nevertheless, sober analysis of this great engagement throws up several complex conclusions. Of particular significance was the reaction of Admiral Sir Max Horton, the intelligent and resourceful Commander of the Western Approaches. He interviewed the luckless and inexperienced Commander of HX229, G J Luther, immediately on his return to Liverpool. Luther left the interview a relieved and, in the circumstances, a fairly happy man. Horton was a ruthless commander but not one who would readily look for scapegoats in a contest between unevenly matched combatants. He had quickly concluded that, while that week in March had been in his own words "one of the blackest on the sea", it had also been a real turning point. Intelligence later revealed that the depressed and frustrated convoy captains had, in fact, damaged no less than seven U-boats, while the huge air attack carried out in response to the destruction of the convoy had damaged a further seven U-boats (albeit some of them very lightly) and sunk two with no survivors.

On the 6th May 1945 the Mosquitos of the RAF coastal command made one of their longest daylight trips to carry out this attack on U-boats. Hits were obtained on 3 fully surfaced U-boats and a minesweeper. This picture shows *U2534* under fire from the Mosquitos.
(Imperial War Museum)

1943: The crew of a destroyed U-boat can be seen clambouring on board a British vessel. *(Imperial War Museum)*

The next two convoys to leave the American seaboard were opposed by 32 U-boats but suffered only one loss. That may have been a freak result, but it provided a psychological uplift for the escorts and convoys.

The 50th Anniversary of the Battle of the Atlantic is commemorated in May 1993. That month in 1943, 60 U-boats in three packs attacked the convoy ON55 returning from the United Kingdom to the United States. Three ships were quickly sunk. Fog descended the following night but this also increased the escorts' radar advantage. Two U-boats rammed each other, a further two were rammed by the escorts and three were destroyed with depth charges. Seven U-boats were lost in total, against 12 merchantmen sunk. Doenitz was reported as describing this as intolerable. He went on to calculate that May 1943 had cost a U-boat for every 10,000 tons of Allied shipping. The year before, in the "happy" time, the loss of one U-boat per 100,000 tons of shipping was the expected score. His final loss count for the month was calculated as 34 U- boats. This was a rate of destruction beyond the power of the German naval construction industry to make good.

The U-boat campaign dragged on after the climatic months of 1943. Horton declined promotion to pursue what was, for him, a personal crusade against Doenitz and the U-boats.

A Technical War

The Atlantic campaign was unique in the technical range and complexity of the weapons and tactics employed, the scale of the war, the use of intelligence and the close control and direction from land-based command centres. Any dispassionate analysis must show, however, that a grasp of the strategic implications of the new technology was sadly lacking in the Admiralty of the

1930s. Until 1916 war at sea had always been between surface ships of rival navies. The British Navy had persisted for most of the 1930s in regarding the 1916 - 1918 submarine campaign as an abberation and the submarine threat as a distraction. The proper business of a Lord High Admiral was to deal with big ships and big guns, and to dream of a new Trafalgar. By the late 1930s the ablest anti-submarine tactician, Commander F J Walker, regarded his effective naval career as at an end. He and his fellow experts were regarded as marginal to Naval policy. It was not just that the threat from submarines was not recognised but that the destructive potential of aircraft against surface ships was only belatedly appreciated. There was a particularly farcical fleet exercise before the outbreak of war, when a radar controlled drone target plane circled the assembled might of the British Navy which blazed away in a pyrotechnic display for over two hours with all guns and failed to scratch the surface of the slow moving target. As war was declared a crash programme was initiatied to supply the fleet with bought-in Swedish- designed anti-aircraft designs.

1945: The British hero class destroyer *HMS Hotspur,* leaving the Gladstone Dock. *(Imperial War Museum)*

The obsession with big ships meant that, in essence, smaller ships were primarily regarded as adjuncts, a protective screen for the battleships. The basic small naval ship was a destroyer, not particularly suited to slow-moving convoy work, expensive to build and expensive to man. Mention has already been made of the desperate attempt to make good the large deficiency in convoy escorts at the beginning of the Second World War, with the adaptation for the Atlantic convoy routes of the old whale catcher design of the Smith's Dock Company of Middlesborough. The basic design remained more or less unchanged throughout the war except that the mast was moved further aft. These ships with their bizarre pedigree cost under £100,000 each. As First Sea Lord at the beginning of the war Churchill had ordered another 30 in addition to the 50 or so already ordered; eventually nearly 300 were to be built. On 12 September 1939, Churchill described the new corvettes as the "cheap and nasties" (cheap to the Allies, but nasty to the U-boats). They were armed with a single 4" gun, a varying number of light anti-aircraft weapons and were capable of carrying a considerable number of depth charges. To the corvettes were added ex-American four-funnelled First World War destroyers. While these were fast, they were as uncomfortable as the corvettes. In addition they were poor anti-submarine ships as they were designed for surface battle, not anti-submarine warfare. It was not until 1942 that a purpose-built escort was in service. This was the frigate - a long-distance ship, faster than the corvette and capable of the corvette's anti-submarine role. All-in-all, convoy escorts were a motley bunch of ships with largely amateur sailors. They were normally manned by the Royal Navy Volunteer Reserves who were "hostilities only" seamen. For example, in the disaster of HX229/SC122, the estimate is that only one fifth of the naval officers involved were regulars and a significant number of these had never sailed before 1939. Intense loyalties developed within these small ships and it is still moving to hear the reminiscences of the escort groups and of the powerful bonds that remain 50 years on.

1943: *HMS Wildgoose* and *HMS Starling* (nearer the camera) in Gladstone Dock. *Starling* had rammed and sunk a U-boat prior to return to port. *(Imperial War Museum)*

The escorts' main aid to battle was ASDIC or sonar - the sounding device fitted underneath a ship's hull. This used sound echos to find the range and direction of a submarine. There were distinct operational drawbacks in that ASDIC was inadequate in determining the depth of a submarine and at close range, when a depth charging attack was about to take place, it was not effective at all. ASDIC was always prone to false readings caused by the seabed in shallow water and even by changes in water temperature. In practice ships could "search" with a narrow beam at a fixed angle at ranges between 200 yards and a mile. Moreoever, rough water and a speed over 8 knots could cause serious disruption. At the start of the war the main, indeed only, weapon against a submerged submarine was a crude depth charge device dropped over the stern of a ship. The depths at which the charge exploded had to be set by hand and on the basis of inadequate ASDIC readings of the estimated depth of the submarine - and by guesswork. The early success rate (measured by submarines sunk) was very low, although the profound psychological impact upon a submarine, effectively blind under water, of a nearby explosion, even where damage was non-existent or minimal, could never be underestimated.

A winter convoy - a destroyer dropping a depth charge. *(Imperial War Museum)*

Throughout the war the depth charge, with all its inadequacies, remained the main anti-submarine weapon. Anti-submarine mortars were developed and one - the Hedgehog - saw general service. In 1944 an extremely efficient heavy mortar - the Squid - improved the kill rate dramatically to 50% for each attack - but it came too late in the war to have significant impact. The kill rate for a single depth charge attack was only 1 in 20.

But it was technique rather than technical superiority which gave the Allies the eventual upper hand. Captain Walker's Second Support Group perfected the method by which a pair of escorts would hunt a submarine in tandem - one would use ASDIC whilst the other would make the depth charging runs. Interestingly Walker was an advocate of the ancient Greek "trireme" technique of ramming - and used it with considerable personal success.

However, the change of the Allies' fortune in the early summer of 1943 was coterminus with the closure of the air-gap in mid-Atlantic. As noted earlier U-boat success was very closely linked to the ability to act, not as a submarine, but as a surface torpedo boat with the capability to submerge when necessary. It was not until late in the war that U-boats could exceed 6/7 knots submerged. Until the development of the "schnorkel" breathing tube, underwater sailing was itself restricted by air supply, and the capacity for the batteries to provide power without recharging. Aircraft properly used were just as significant in the destruction of U-boats as were escorts attached to convoys or to detached support groups such as Walker's. Not until 1942 did the Allies use air cover to full effect. At this stage in the war there was a dramatic technical improvement with the introduction of an extremely powerful aircraft-launched depth charge, effective air base search radar accompanied, at night, by a very high-powered search light system (the "Lee Light").

Technical developments, however, were not all one way. Convoys themselves were at risk from Brittany-based reconnaisance and attack aircraft. Moreover just as the Allies were taking effective aircraft measures against the U-boats in 1942, the submarines were equipped with a very effective receiver which was able to pick up the radar signals used by the Allied aircraft. Throughout the war German torpedo design and reliability improved dramatically. Of particular impact against convoys was the FAT torpedo which was programmed to reverse course within a moving convoy and make several passes. Similarly there were constant developments in the U-boats themselves. There were nine main U-boat types with upwards of 20 variations. The standard propulsion was by diesel engine with the revolutionary "Walter" boats emerging as the war ended.

One element of the Allied campaign was a total failure: the attempt to bomb the U-boat base in Brittany. Although at one point the RAF deployed up to a fifth of its force in an attack, the only result was to flatten civilian areas around the U-boat pens, causing thousands of French casualties and much resentment. There is no evidence of any submarine being damaged. Hitler had personally instructed that the U-boat pens should be protected with reinforced concrete, four metres thick. At the beginning of 1943 10,000 tons of bombs were dropped to no military effect whatsoever.

The Battle of the Atlantic was the first extended naval campaign to be controlled directly by land-based commanders. British Command in Derby House and the German Command in the Kerneval Chateau were both dependent on radio control for the direction of their respective forces and radio transmission could betray information about the strength and position of the opposing forces. It was radio intelligence which provided the strategic key to the conduct of the campaign. Throughout the war, radio silence had to take second place to strategic command and U-boat transmissions provided both British and American listeners with basic information for the re-routing of convoys. But this basic radio intelligence was encoded and it was a massive feat on both sides to break the codes used. This was "the great game of radio warfare" and it is probable that the Germans were ahead in this aspect of the campaign. For most of the war the German B-Dienst were able to read the Royal Navy's coded signals. The Royal Navy, however, was baffled by the German Navy's "shark" key which was used to control U-boats in 1942, when shipping losses were at their worst. Although that code was broken in December 1942, minor changes made it unreadable in March 1943 and this undoubtedly contributed to the disasters of convoys HX229 and SC122.

The real significance of radio communication intelligence throughout the campaign is the role played by the naval planners in the central headquarters. Even without fully decoding material the control room at Derby House managed to redirect well over half of all convoys away from suspected wolf pack traps. On both sides the war at sea was controlled from land.

The Merchant Ships and Seamen

By 1942 after three years of war the Cabinet's "Atlantic Committee" had finally brought the docks under control with dock employment classed as a national service with a weekly wage. Government management of the merchant navy on the other hand was never as complete as the requirements of total war dictated. Organisation of the Merchant Navy was bedevilled by ad hoc regulation and crisis response. The central issue of control was addressed only by layer upon layer of complex regulation. The means of supply and the survival of the United Kingdom were in the hands of privately-owned shipping companies throughout the war, although they acted under Government direction. The seamen who manned the merchant ships remained employees of the ship-owners.

Merchant seamen being rescued after being torpedoed. They are picked up by a British rescue ship. *(Imperial War Museum)*

Nearly 30,000 seamen died on British merchant ships as a direct result of enemy actions. Several thousands more died as an indirect result, for example, in blackout collisions at sea. The death rate was higher than in any of the armed services. Over 4,800 ships were lost.

At the start of war the merchant fleet was not in a good condition. British ships tended to be backward technologically with few oil burners. Coal was preferred as a cheap fuel but it made for far slower ships in convoy. Just under 200,000 men were employed in the merchant marine, 140,000 were British citizens and there were 10,000 Europeans and 50,000 non-Europeans, mainly Indian. Preparations and training for war were both tardy and inadequate. In 1937 gunnery training courses were established in the ports but there was no effective compulsion upon the ship-owners to have crews trained and at the start of war there is no evidence of any real policy to arm the merchant ships.

Requisitioning of ships began at the outbreak of the war. It was a strange system - a form of compulsory hire. Rates of hire were fixed by the Government to cover owners' costs, provide an adequate allowance for depreciation and to give a reasonable return on capital. For passenger ships of 5,000 tons and over requisitioned as troop ships, the rates fixed to operate from 1 March 1942 were between 10s 5d and 13s 7d per ton per month. For cargo ships rates were to vary between 7s 9d and 8s. If ships were sunk, the Government's insurance scheme paid out not the increased value that the ship had acquired by surviving so far, but by paying the owner enough for a replacement to be used on further convoy duty. For liners, the owners were allowed 5% return on capital and 5% cover for depreciation. Under the ship building scheme there was effectively a heavy subsidy on new build. On the face of it the owners could not lose. Their ships, profits and losses were all underwritten by the Government and as new ships were built they were allotted to ship-owners, under generous loan arrangements. The whole system of war-time merchant navy management created huge unresolved tensions. The Government through the port authorities directed the ships and controlled the cargoes, but the ship-owners still provided the crew, bunkers and stores and were supposed to carry out repairs and be responsible for the fitness of the boat. As pressure for quick turn-around of ships intensified, there was every incentive for the owner to neglect safety requirements in the interests, of course, of national survival. There are stories of seamen with no experience in rescue procedures or ship evacuation procedures, and of losses of life due not to a ship being torpedoed but to inadequate training. Stories too of poorly maintained rescue boats and even of lifeboats nailed onto ships to stop them rocking.

Captains of Merchant Ships at a convoy conference in Derby House. These conferences took place before each convoy. *(Imperial War Museum)*

The manning of vessels was the ship-owners' responsibility but wartime regulation of labour restricted real freedom of labour movement. On 8 May 1941 the Essential Work Order provided for continuity of employment and payment whilst waiting for a ship; longer leave on pay and free travel on leave; a Merchant Navy resource pool of officers and men at all times available for appointment to ships, and registration of all those who had left the sea since 1936. This was conscription in all but name: a "civilian" occupation with a death rate already exceeding that of any of the armed services. At the end of every sea-going engagement every officer and man, unless immediately re-engaged by some employer, passed automatically into a Merchant Navy Resource Pool controlled by the Shipping Federation. In practice, a man would be given "two refusals" of ships before being assigned to a third and the war did at least guarantee employment and the prospect of goods abroad which were not available in rationed war-torn Britain. The general impression is of a fairly philosophical attitude, and relaxed fatalism amongst seamen, but this, however, did not extend to the Arctic convoys. Russia had no attractions, no luxuries on offer, just incredible cold and ice packs, appalling weather conditions and constant threat from U-boat and aircraft.

The system of compulsion chafed on individuals and as the war progressed there was an increase in prosecutions on Merseyside for refusal to obey orders and for desertion. The war did nothing to lessen the caste-like division between owners and crews and between officers and men. Tony Lane's detailed perceptive analysis of the experiences of war of merchant seamen "The Merchant Seaman's War" makes the convincing point that "... the everyday experience was predominantly one of familiar routines within which war was an interruption from outside".

Merchantmen in Convoy

As far as Merchantmen were concerned the biggest interruption to their daily routines tended to be, not the Germans, but the Royal Navy and the convoy system. The class differences between officers and crews in merchant ships were reflected in the very different milieu of officers in the two services. At times it seemed that the only attitude in common between the two navies was a mutual contempt. If anything that contempt was stronger on the Merchant Navy side - officers and crew regarded themselves simply as far more competent sailors.

The theory of convoy is an ancient one stretching back to the Romans. In its Second World War variant it would typically consist of up to 60 merchant ships in roughly 10 columns with about 1,000 yards between the columns stretching from front to rear about five miles. Round the convoy the Naval escorts would form a protective screen. Until 1943, however, the escort screen could often be very thin as Horton struggled with his limited resources. Every convoy was directed by the Admiralty.

1943: A typical Atlantic convoy as seen from an aircraft of Coastal Command.
(Imperial War Museum)

The cultural differences between Navy and the shipping trade were unbridgeable. Convoy commanders were normally retired Admirals used to a hierarchical command structure. Merchant captains were normally answerable only to the ship-owner, God and the Board of Trade - if a ship sank. Naval officers were used to Fleet manoeuvres, Merchant Captains never sailed in close company and were used to altering route to avoid bad weather. Friction was endless with independently-minded captains frequently breaking convoy discipline and in one case abandoning the convoy altogether for a fast run home. For the Royal Navy, war was often a question of command structure communication and corporate activity. Tony Lane sums up the attitude of merchant seafarers "... notably inward looking and carrying with them a strong sense of the war not being theirs. The war did not therefore, in their perception of it, require fundamental changes in their ways of thinking and acting. On the other hand, the nation to which they belonged and in which they had a stake was under threat and therefore needed to be defended. But that only required of them that they continue to do their job. They did, and so did millions of others. When seafarers set the war aside and hoped for its end, the limit of their aspirations was the restoration of the remembered rhythms of the peace time voyage".

Captain F J "Johnny" Walker - A Hero for the Time

War exposed the people of Bootle to a new world outside, which was totally alien to the experience of them all. It was a world of intermittent saturation bombing, devastation of living and working space, of violent death. It was not the food and clothing rationing, the physical deprivation and boredom of war that troubles people in the contemporary accounts. Bootle accepted poverty as entirely natural. It was the arbitrary nature of the threat to life and with it the vaguely perceived external threat to the sense of identity. It was not that this sense of identity was particularly national in its scope and there is not a shred of evidence that the people of Bootle felt they were fighting for "democracy". Like most British people they rarely articulated what they were fighting for. When the bombs fell, the people of Bootle fought with varying degrees of heroism and occasionally cowardice for their families, their relatives, friends or neighbours and for their particular part of the world or because it was their job to fight. They fought for remarkably ordinary things and the fight was against chaos and physical destruction.

It is possible that it was the very grimness of the war in Bootle that caused the adoption of Captain F J "Johnny" Walker as the archetypal hero. Walker and his support groups brought excitement, heroic action, attack and not defence. Until the arrival of Walker, Bootle had known only deprivation, bombing and censored press accounts of grave shipping losses in the Atlantic convoys - and word of mouth accounts of painful human loss in the sinkings. There was no particular excitement and little glow in a successful convoy - after all successful convoys were essentially negative - only a small number of ships were lost. Walker was a very successful commander - but perhaps even more important - he changed the way the people of Bootle saw the war.

Walker's career, until the outbreak of war, was decidedly ordinary. Following a family tradition he joined the navy in 1913 and proved a very able cadet. He saw active service in the Great War, with the Second Battle Squadron of the Grand Fleet aboard the battleship *HMS Ajax*. During the inter-war years, he found himself in the very unfashionable area of anti-submarine warfare. For a period of more than a decade he was one of the few anti-submarine specialists in the navy spending a good deal of time at the anti-submarine school, Portland, of ASDIC fame. In 1926 he was the anti-submarine officer of the Atlantic Fleet and then of the Mediterranean Fleet, posts which were decidedly not reserved for those destined for the higher reaches of the Navy. He was appointed commanding officer of *HMS Shikari* and then the *Falmouth* but contemplated the end of his naval career when he was returned to the Portland training school prior to the Second World War. It seems that he was not a particularly popular man and criticism of his ability was recorded at the Admiralty - one report described him as lacking powers of leadership. War rescued Walker from career oblivion. In 1940 he was appointed Operations Staff Officer to Admiral Ramsey and then in October 1941 to sea service as commander of the 36th Escort Group raising his flag in the sloop *HMS Stork*, whose home base was the Gladstone Dock complex. Thus began the intimate and unlikely associations between the northern working class town and its adopted hero - the career naval officer, a God-fearing, Church-going family man who took a positive delight in killing in what was for him a self-evidently good cause. The 36th Escort Group was initially engaged in escorting Gibraltar- bound convoys and Walker used these runs to train and drill the convoy escorts to act as a team. The first drill was called "Buttercup", but after he worked the drills up at Derby House they became known as the "Fruit" drills. Walker was fortunate in that his early convoys were well supplied with escorts and he instinctively adopted aggressive tactics to such effect that four U-boats were confirmed sunk. At a subsequent Admiralty meeting he became the first front line sailor of substance to stress the importance of co-ordinated defence incorporating land-based and carrier based air cover. Walker's skills were recognised by Admiral Horton and despite the fact that he had hitherto been passed over for promotion and was well beyond "the promotion zone in seniority" he was specially promoted to Captain.

1943: Captain F.J. Walker, DSO, RN, addresses the men of *HMS Wildgoose* after a successful patrol where two U-boats were destroyed in the space of nine hours. *(Imperial War Museum)*

The Second Support Group was established in April 1943 immediately after the disasters of convoys SC122 and HX229. The six ships were purpose-built long range anti-submarine attack ships - sloops - and the Group was given an offensive role rather than defensive convoy duties. It is perhaps more accurate to say that Horton's intention was to provide better defence for convoys by disrupting the U-boats own attack methods. Using Derby House real time intelligence the Group would actively hunt down submarine packs or come to the aid of any convoy under severe pressure. At the heart of the attack technique was a development of the "Buttercup" drill with sloops acting in tandem. One ship would provide locational guidance by ASDIC as to a U-boat's whereabouts, the other would saturate the identified area with depth charges. This technique required constant practice and a tremendous degree of understanding between captains. However, when properly used it overcame one of the main problems of ASDIC, its ineffectiveness when a ship was in close proximity to a submarine, when it was in the very act of depth-charging.

The Group's successes exceeded all expectations. Walker's constant drilling meant that soon all ships could act as a single unit and "hold the ring" around a trapped U-boat. The Bay of Biscay proved the happy hunting ground - Walker's own phrase unconsciously echoing the U-boats "happy time". The Bay covered the entrances to the U-boat pens in Brittany. In all the Second Support Group destroyed 21 submarines and played a major role in shifting the balance of the Battle of the Atlantic.

The Group's exploits were avidly followed in the home port and the sailors appropriately feted. Walker himself was guest of honour in the Town Hall on each return to harbour. Apocryphally perhaps he is reported to have slept regularly in the Town Hall, but three different locations are given - attic, cellar and Mayor's parlour. This man passed over for promotion and faintly damned as a poor leader before the war was clearly worshipped by his men and adored by the people of Bootle. The stories abound and the gestures captured the mood of the time.

Walker could drink a pint of beer standing on his head. Walker's reports to Derby House were racy, simple, patriotic and reminiscent of "the Great Game" of a former era. "This is typical of Walker", Sir Max Horton said of one of them. "A nice bright breezy report, even if the metaphors are a bit mixed. All huntin', shootin' and fishin' with a little cricket thrown in for good measure". Walker thrilled at the chase and was brutal and blood-thirsty at the kill:

1944: Captain Walker shouts encouragement to the sloop *Woodpecker*. The 1944 Admiralty press release states that he was saying: "Go on *Woodpecker*, do your stuff, and beat the pants off her ..." as it goes into the attack.
(Imperial War Museum)

"Eventually I managed to ram her just before the conning tower from an angle of about 20 deg on her starboard quarter, and roll her over. She hung for a few seconds on the bow and again on the Asdic dome and then scraped aft were she was greeted by a 10 charge pattern (9 only fired) at shallowest settings. I was informed that a Bosch in the water, holding up his arms and crying "Kamerade", receive the contents of the thrower in his face instead."

Walker was self-effacing and spoke the slightly unreal language of a modest hero, "... I do not think I am an ace U-boat killer", he said "... this kind of warfare is not the sort that has one man as its ace protagonist. Fighting U-boats is very much like playing football or any other sort of game. You have a team of one thousand men, any one of whom can wreck the whole show if he doesn't do his whole job properly. Every man has his own job to do - I am merely the head of the affair, so please don't call me U-boat killer number one. That formidable character is one thousand British tars."

Walker would play "A hunting we will go" during each submarine attack and was trying out a special recording of the tune a few days before he died. Walker without a trace of apparent arrogance, irony or mockery was only the third commander in naval history to hoist "the General Chase" signal in any engagement, following Drake's pursuit of the Armada up the Channel and Nelson's attack upon the French fleet at the Battle of the Nile.

1944: The Second Support Group's successful patrol when 6 U-boats were sunk. The press release stated: "It shows Captain Walker on the bridge taking a bearing on a submerged U-boat on receiving a report - "Echo 180 degrees - sir". *(Imperial War Museum)*

The return of *HMS Starling* to Liverpool, with Captain F.J. Walker standing on the bridge mounting after the record breaking U-boat hunt in which six enemy submarines were destroyed by the Second Support Group. Marine bands and massed crowds cheer the homecoming.
(Imperial War Museum)

In 1944, only months before his early death from overwork, there were unparalleled scenes in the Gladstone Dock on the Group's return. Six U-boats had been destroyed in a single patrol, a tremendous feat of arms. As the Group sailed in line ahead up the Mersey and into the Canada Basin the quays were crowded with cheering sailors from the convoy escorts and the battleship *King George V*. As *Starling* and *Kite* berthed side-by-side in a Gladstone branch dock a great crowd of Bootle citizens joined the sailors. The First Sea Lord reviewed the Group with Sir Max Horton before riotous celebrations in the town.

When Walker died the funeral service was conducted in the Liverpool Cathedral. Horton read the oration "... the Western Approaches shall be his tomb", and the gun carriage cortege proceeded to the Pier Head at a slow march. Captain F J "Johnny" Walker the Royal Navy's greatest front line anti-submarine tactician and the greatest hero of the Battle of the Atlantic was buried at sea in sight of the Bootle Docks.

AFTERWORD

Personal Wars

George Lunt

When war broke out I was in the Merchant Navy. When I got home to Liverpool, I was paid off and went to put my cards in the "dole" - which we used to do before the war. I was offered a card and told I'd be sailing the following morning. Eight months away - home two days and away again. I said no. I'd had my name down at the Dock Board for ten years and each time I came home from sea I'd go down to see if they wanted me. It was a good job on the docks pre-war. When I got there they said they'd been waiting for me and I started the following Monday. I became a dock gateman at Gladstone Dock.

My responsibilities were the sluices, the paddles, and opening the gates. The lock of the Gladstone was 1000 feet which meant we could get the big ships in. It could take any ship at all. The ship coming through the gates would be for Gladstone. If they were for Alexandra or Langton they had to come through Hornby lock.

Derby House used to regulate berths for the convoys waiting at the Bar and it was up to the owners to notify the dock. We knew how many to expect at Gladstone.

I've seen about 30 destroyers and corvettes in the Gladstone Dock. They were priority. At times five or six troop ships would be in the Gladstone Dock - the *Mauretania, Aquitania* and so on. Cargoes had lower priority. The turn around depended on the dockers. They used to load the cargo onto trains and take them out - quick transport. The trains used to keep going during the raids.

During the blackout there wasn't a light on the docks. You couldn't be too careful - dozens fell in. I fell in the dock. I shouted and they came to the side of Hornby Dock. One said "What are you doing there?" I said "What do you think I'm doing here?" "Get out you soft bugger" he said. "Get out the way you got in", and I had to swim to the ladder - with boots, overcoat - full uniform on.

I tried to get off the docks and into the navy or the merchant section. We used to see all the troops going out during the war - three or four of us on the docks decided we'd try and get away but they had us up before the Harbour Master - and he said "You try and get away ..... if you can". We were an essential service you see.

Frank H

June 1941. Just 15 years old - like so many other young men at the time, I ran away from home. I managed to get a job as a ship's watchman - working days, earning enough to survive.

Whilst acting as watchman on the *S S Argos Hill,* I approached the Bosun and was told to stay on board when the ship sailed. We anchored near to the Bar where I was signed-on as an Ordinary Seaman, and fitted out with sea-going gear (to be charged against my earnings).

I was put on the middle watch, and first night out given first "trick" on the wheel. Thank the Lord one of the Able Seamen stood behind me telling me what to do. I learned very rapidly on the ship and have much to be grateful for to the crew who showed great patience.

This first trip was to New York, where we tied up at Pier 90. We were allowed a sub of £5. The Bosun borrowed 5 "bucks" from me, went ashore and never appeared again. It was only after we sailed homeward that we found out he had "tapped" nearly every crew member and had a few hundred dollars when he "jumped ship".

The homeward journey was uneventful, other than, shortly after joining the convoy, the skipper ordered "hard-a-starboard" and we went round in circles until the convoy disappeared. We got home 2 days before the convoy! Leave next, then I signed on at the Merchant navy pool.

The *S S Merylyn* next - tons of cement poured into the fore-peak - a dead give away. Only a ship bound for Russia would need to strengthen her bows in this way against ice.

Off to Birkenhead to load with a mixed bag of cargo - tanks; arms; petrol; sugar - a fairly lethal combination all round.

We joined a fair-sized convoy to Murmansk. The weather was vicious - bitterly cold causing a gradual build-up of ice which covered the ship.

The only cold weather gear which was issued to us was a duffle coat (which "cracked" as if lined with paper, when it got cold) and two pairs of seaboat socks. The ladies who knitted "comforts" for seamen were silently thanked every day, for woollen jerseys, socks, balaclavas, gloves and mittens. They did a wonderful job in keeping us warm.

Other than the weather, the trip was fairly routine, except for one incident. At 1 am one of the tanks (Valentines I think) broke loose in No 2 hatch between docks. Believe me it's no joke trying to strip off 8 inches of ice from the hatch cover, in order to get below to re-secure the runaway tank.

After leave at home I reported to the "Pool" and was signed on to a tanker *M V Dromus* which was supposedly berthed at Stanlow. I, together with the new crew members, was told to report to a tug the following morning, which was to drop us at Stanlow.

What a con! Instead of turning up-river,, the tug turned down-river and near the Bar, the *M V Dromus* firmly at anchor, awaiting a US-bound convoy. I must say, it was a good, clean, well-found ship - well and smoothly run.

We sailed in convoy to Halifax, Nova Scotia and split up. The *Dromus* heading for New York, we were intending to go through the Cape Cod canal and we approached the canal in fairly thick fog, foghorns blowing and ships bells ringing all around us. As we approached the mouth of the canal, a destroyer, heading north at a fairly high speed, came out of the canal and hit us on the port side, causing some damage. Consequently, on arrival at New York, the ship went into dry dock and all the crew were sent ashore.

From New York we sailed to Marcus Hook off the Delaware loaded with 100 octane aviation spirit a convoy back to Long Island sound. This stretch of the US east coast was a veritable U-boat alley for a while, a large number of ships being lost.

This trip turned out to be my last true North Atlantic convoy as from August 1942 to October 1944 my service was spent trooping in the South Atlantic and Indian Oceans.

After my leave I was sent by the "Pool" to the Forces Recruiting Office in Renshaw Street and was conscripted into the army which I then made my career, retiring on a pension in June 1968.

Winifred Toale

When the war broke out I was seven years of age and living in Talbot Street, near the top of Marsh Lane.

Being a main thoroughfare it couldn't have any shelters built in the road, so before the shelter was built in our back yard we used to use the cellars of the shops on Marsh Lane. Dad was a Merchant Seaman. He came home one night during a raid and found our mother, with us five chicks sheltering under the stairs. Dad, took a child under each arm - and up the street we went to the shop cellar.

I vividly remember jumping over flares as they dropped all around us. We could hear the drone of the planes but we couldn't look up, simply because we were trying to dodge the flares. We could hear the noise of the guns - the ack ack.

Down into the cellar we went. It was a dark, damp, horrible place - but it was safe and it was our air raid shelter for quite some time. We were frightened, but as children we didn't know what we were frightened of. The shelter was bombed. It was full of people when it was hit. We all got upstairs - we all got out. I remember what I thought were army girls, with their coats off, helping us to get out.

When we did get out, the siding opposite Marsh Lane had been hit. There was a coal yard there with nothing but a little hut built on it and because of the open space chickens, horses and cows were kept there. Can you imagine - when it was hit and went on fire - all the animals running down the road. Mostly they ran down Talbot Street as this was right opposite. It wasn't funny to me - the wails of those animals running for dear life - it was nightmarish.

We were a close knit family. My mother never wanted us to be evacuated, she liked to think we were within ear shot or eyesight. When the raids got particularly bad, and Bootle was being bombarded, I remember we went to St James' School and there we had to climb into meat wagons. They shut the doors and you couldn't see anything - arms and legs were everywhere. We were driven to the outskirts - taken out at night and returned the following morning.

We used to go to Marsh Lane Slipper Baths. On one of our visits we learned that behind the "green" wooden doors were kept the dead bodies of air raid casualties - the mortuary. My sister's friend was as fascinated as we were scared and said how she wished she could have a look behind the doors. Not long after our visit to the baths, her house was bombed. Her younger brother had had an accident on his leg and it was in plaster-of-paris. To my knowledge the entire family lost their lives sheltering under the stairs. Searching through the debris two women thought they had a "find" of a white tablecloth - which turned out to be the plastered leg. Our friend's wish had been granted.

"Lord Haw Haw" delighted in informing the residents of Bootle "The kisses on your windows won't save you" - but they did!

I can remember being hungry. Food was plain. The flour was grey, coarse, horrible. We had only scrapings of butter or margarine to put on the bread. My father sometimes used to bring home white flour, or a tin of pineapple. Once he brought a 56 lb pack of butter - nobody had fridges then so my mother went up and down the road giving out the butter to neighbours. We thought we were fortunate.

John Flaherty

I was six when war broke out. I lived in Boswell Street near to the Seaforth end of the docks. In those days young lads did one of two things - they went to sea or worked on the docks.

My earliest recollection of the war is receiving my gas mask - we all had one. It had to be carried everywhere - to school and back. We were issued with little cardboard boxes in which to keep them. The babies had Mickey Mouse gas masks. The next thing I remember is having an air raid shelter built in the back yard. It was just four walls and a concrete roof. You had to supply your own door. How they thought we'd be safe in there without a door on the thing - I don't know. Usually it was one shelter per family, but they also built large ones in the streets, for the communities - where they couldn't be built in the back yards.

My father was never with us. He worked on the docks. He was also a warden, so when he wasn't on the docks, he'd don his tin hat and go out to patrol the streets. The air raid shelter was just for my mother, my sisters and me. One of our neighbours - Mrs Lloyd - used to come in with us with her baby son. Her husband was away in the merchant navy. She was the life and soul of the party - so organised. She had us drawing and playing lots of games. She kept our minds occupied. Everyone was scared - but Mrs Lloyd was a treasure.

You'd hear the bombs coming down. You'd hear the whistling and then wait for the bang - it was very frightening. The things of war became a way of life - the standpipes in the street, the gas masks. Emergency water pipes would appear along the edge of the pavements after a bad night's raid.

You'd be issued with brown tape to place crosses on the windows in an effort to save them from shattering in a blast. The glass was never replaced, just a white canvas to cover the hole. You couldn't get a pane of glass. You got used to the devastation - to us kids it was like a big playground. We used to collect pieces of the incendiary bombs and store them up in a tin box. It became a great game - something to swap with friends.

School was a confusing place. There were unexploded bombs at my school so we had to travel to other schools for our lessons. St Joan of Arc School - there was an American camp next to it - on Rimrose Road. I remember one time there were Italian prisoners of war there - what a fascination for us kids.

I lost friends in the raids. You'd go in to school after a raid and there'd be spaces in the classroom. We knew what had happened.

I was never evacuated before the May Blitz - but afterwards I was. Just before the Blitz, wagons started to come along and pick up families, around 6.00 pm, and they'd be taken out to the countryside. You'd sleep in halls or on straw and then come back the following morning. It was just "going away for the night".

After the blitz we were evacuated. My mother came with us. This was an unhappy time for the whole family. My father had to stay to work on the docks. We went to Southport. We weren't allowed to mix with children from the other families. At the house we were made to feel different, even at school we were segregated. A lot of evacuees were treated very badly - a friend of mine was beaten. I and my sisters had our mother - a lot of the evacuees did not.

We had to queue for everything. We all had ration books but we still had to queue. Saturday was a busy day for our family. Each of us would be assigned to different queues for the rations. As I got older, I'd help dad in getting the coal ration.

Bernard Baxter

I was 16 years old when I started work on the tugs in 1942. Our tug was called the *Ceemore* - it was one of Furness Withy's tugs. I was the tug "boy" - what you might call an apprentice. We had to do everything - scrub the decks, scrub the cabins, clean the brasses - everything. The Captain used to go around with a torch - looking under the buckets, everywhere - checking it all.

A big ship had to have the tugs to stop it from smashing against the sides of the lock. The larger ships in the convoys couldn't get in to the docks further up river, so they had to go into the Bootle end. If they went into the Gladstone they couldn't get to any other dock.

Hornby Dock was the Furness Withy berth mostly holding the meat boats. Earlier in the war the entrance to the Hornby Dock was bombed. To get to the Bootle docks ships had to enter the Sandon basin, then come through the dock complex. The docks were busy. Sometimes there'd be two or three ships - one waiting for the other to be away. A lot of cargo was loaded on to barges and went up the canal.

Work dependend on the tides. Men had to go out at each high water - every twelve hours. You may be out six - eight hours and then have to get out a few hours later, for the next tide.

There was no way of knowing whether there were any mines in the river until something hit one. One tug, going out to pick up a ship, hit a mine and blew up. They used to have trawlers to sweep the area.

The tugs used to fire watch and some of them had pumps - say one every so often - so that if anything happened you could get alongside the ship from the dock side.

We nearly always knew somebody who was working on the ship. They'd pass out tins of corned beef, or crab or whatever. One time, we were waiting alongside ship for the water to "level". Someone on the ship popped his head out and was asked if he knew a certain bloke. "How about some grub" he was asked. Something like an hour later the bloke appears and shouts from the ship, 20 foot up, "... throw us a line". We threw the line, he tied a packet to it and pulled it back. Egg sandwiches - half a million of them. He must have been standing in the cookhouse boiling eggs.

We knew where the ships were going. We were asked not to tell. We didn't know the names of the (Royal) Navy ships. One time we went out to meet a ship - an "escort carrier" - no name on it. When we got out there we shouted "What ship is it?" The Captain was making gestures on the deck, waving his arms about. It was *HMS Fencer.* I worked on the tugs for a while - until I joined the army and the parachute regiment - where I was when the war ended.

Harold Walker

I started my service with the Merchant Navy six weeks after I left school, at the age of 14.

I was a "ship's boy". My first voyage was in the *RMS Montclare* in June 1939. It was common for boys of my age to be on board ships. We were asked if we wanted to continue with service (when war broke out). I chose to stay. I had no particular responsibility. Just general work. We had some survival training after the war broke out - what to do when the ship was torpedoed - the procedure to release the lifeboat. The training was very inadequate - really we learnt by example. On one ship, the *Orbertha,* there were "double banked" lifeboats - one on top of the other. The top one was sound - the bottom one was painted to the deck.

Before about mid 1940 the convoys weren't organised. A ship made way the best it could. We'd maybe have air cover for the first three days. After that nothing. We didn't really think of the danger. It was a job. From mid 1940 we got increased salary - war, danger allowance. Wives and mothers would go to the shipping offices to collect their wages. Wages stopped on the day a ship sunk. One ship I was on which sunk, the *Redgate,* got hit at five minutes to midnight. Wages stopped at that time. We were paid £25 compensation for loss of our belongings and wages. The widow's money stopped at the same time. I don't remember much about being hit. I was asleep at the time. I managed to get off the boat and was picked up soon afterwards by the ship's lifeboat. The convoy didn't wait to pick up survivors. We were attacked on a number of voyages, usually for periods of three to five days. Often it was in atrocious weather conditions and it was a nightmare. One of the vessels I served on had a gun - a wooden gun.

At times we transported prisoners of war. I once witnesses the flogging of a German prisoner who had been caught stealing from his fellow prisoners. The Guards in charge were South African troops. We were warned to keep away from the Germans.

I remember returning home after the May Blitz in 1941. We anchored in the middle of nowhere. The crew were paid off and put on a train, for Liverpool.

We'd been informed that bombing had gone on, but we didn't know how complete the devastation was that had taken place.

It was 20 May 1941. I can't describe the trauma of arriving home not knowing if our families or homes were still there - it was tremendous. You just didn't know what to expect. It is sad that the role the Merchantmen played, hasn't had the recognition it deserves. Not a great deal is said about it.

I left the Merchant Navy in 1950.

L Chappell; A West; R Squires; C Hughes

Those first two years of the war were the hardest. Whilst on the *Deptford* we had a very unfortunate occurrence. We were in convoy coming home from Gibraltar. It was a hectic time, we lost several ships. We'd had a lot of contact with U-boats. One night Captain Walker instructed our ship to go to investigate and report a U-boat - so many miles away from the convoy. We went and we ascertained that it was not a U-boat, so we made our way back to the convoy. The fog came down - very bad. As we approached the convoy our submarine detector reported that he'd got a contact, thought it was a submarine. We went, we rammed it. It was Captain Walker's ship - really - the *Stork*. We just missed the stearing gear. We killed two people - two German prisoners of wars. That was convoy HG66.

We had a canteen ashore - at the West Gladstone - with a bar and a chapel. It was called the Flotilla Club. The *Caradoc* was the famous pub - well that was its official name - but all of the sailors knew it as "The Bucket of Blood".

Whenever the lads used to go ashore - they'd go to the *Royal* or the *Caradoc* - coming back to the ship around 11 pm. The dockers would nearly always be working in the north west Gladstone. One night, they were unloading a New Zealand company ship. Frozen lamb.

Next thing the police were on board. They knew the legs of lamb were on board. They found five of them. They never found the sixth - I walked into the Officers' toilets and placed it on the Captain's seat. They wouldn't look there.

We had two mascots on the *Stork* - a cat and a dog. The dog was a mixed breed - word got round it was picked up at sea from a sinking ship. When we came home to the Gladstone nobody would see this dog. It'd leave the ship and it finished up in the town - doing the rounds of the pubs with the lads - but it never missed a trip on the ship. He was called Buster.

Once an enemy ship had been sunk or damaged - the crew in the water were harmless. You'd pick them up as long as you weren't putting your crew in danger. You had to be ruthless - but on the other hand if you had the chance to pick up survivors you did. It was up to the Captain - his own ship and crew's welfare came first.

We used to get these big, long range German planes coming out to the convoy. One pilot knew very good English. He signalled to Walker "Beer in the mess was lovely and cool last night - hope you had a peaceful night".

There was nothing funny about it at the time. The thing was, you'd have such a rough time at sea, you'd be glad to get home - splash out a bit. After a couple of days you'd forget about it all. What used to get us down - a lovely summer's day - we'd be on our way out again - you'd see all the people on New Brighton beach enjoying themselves and you were out there and you didn't know what you were going to face.

George Bryson

I went to sea in 1941 as an indented apprentice. I joined my first ship on 3 November 1941. We got back to Liverpool from the first trip on 25 March 1944. That was 2 years, 4 months, 25 days - I think - without coming home.

Albert Meadham

I joined the Navy in 1941. I was trained in Pwllheli and went in the DEMS - Royal Navy attached to merchant ships. I was a gunner on the merchant ships.

We'd usually work four hours on and eight hours off. When we were in danger zones we'd work four hours on, four hours off. It wasn't easy to relax. In four years I was never on a ship that was hit and I never fired a shot at anything.

The nearest I got to violence was when I went to join a ship at Bootle. When I got there the dock gate had been smashed. The dock was empty and the ship I was to go on was sort of hanging by its mooring ropes. I couldn't get on it at all.

I left the navy at the beginning of 1946.

May Logan

Serving as an air raid warden during the raids on Bootle my sector included the large public shelter in the North Park. Just before Christmas 1940 I was patrolling along Stanley Road, one very dark night, no moon, no stars, and the blackout in operation. As planes passed overhead I heard the whistle of falling bombs and dropped to the floor. I felt the blast as the bombs hit the ground.

Before I could do anything I heard screams coming from the nearby shelter in the park and I ran down the path to the entrance. Lying on the floor screaming was a young woman and people just inside the shelter told me that the woman had been standing on top of the shelter and the blast from the bomb had blown her off. I realised she would have to be taken to the first aid post in the health centre further down the park. I tried to get her on her feet but she fought me off. She was about five feet eight and plump and I was only four feet ten so I could not carry her. There were two young soldiers near the entrance of the shelter and I asked them to help me but they refused. They said they were not risking their lives for a foolish girl. I admit planes were still overhead.

I had no time to argue so I set off running across the park to get help from the warden's post, when suddenly I fell into a large hole. I managed to scramble out and realised that it was the crater made by the bomb the blast of which had blown the girl from the shelter.

Two wardens came to my help and we carried the girl to the first aid post and we laughed when the nurse said she thought I was the casualty as I had blood on my face, hands and knees.

Wilf G

I volunteered for the navy when I was seventeen. We sailed on a training trawler from the Gladstone docks. I was a radar operator. When we got to sea we found that our food stores had been raided by the dockers. They took the best stuff and left us the rubbish like the soya (sawdust) sausages.

Otto von Bulow

Kapitan zur See a.D. *(from a letter written in 1992)*

In the daybreak of the 1st of June 1942 about 300 n m north west of Bermuda "U404" attacked the american freighter *West Notus* by gun fire. The risk to meet an adversary much superior by artillery had to be taken because of shortage of position for torpedo launching. At that time of the war every freighter was well armed and had a trained crew against the little gun of our submarines.

Opening fire "U404" had the good luck to hit the bridge by one of the first shells and flames spread out. Very effective gun fire by a 5 inch calibre was returned and near misses and some splinters hit the sub now running away at full speed zig zagging, when all of a sudden life boats were lowered and ship was abandoned. While two boats were sailing away in good order a third one manned by 5 men was sucked with water and motionless. One of these men, who turned out to be the chief mate of the freighter was requested to come aboard the sub. I welcomed him with handshake and the words "I am so sorry but this is war. I hope it will be soon over and I am sure we will be very good friends". We had a long conversation about ship and cargo and the gun fight, while we were towing the damaged lifeboat towards the boats under sail to hand over the chief mate and his men. Returned to the burning ship we discovered another man hanging in a life-belt, picked him up and took care of his wounded leg and delivered him to the life boats undersails now almost at the horizon.

This rescue work was a matter of course and very simple humanity but it may be of interest in the light of the propaganda against the Germans in those war times. I never heard any "hurrah" of the crew when a ship had been torpedoed and sunken.

(From a second letter written in 1992 recalling the sinking of HMS Veteran)

The sinking of *HMS Veteran* on 26th September 1942 will always be a date for me to memorize this terrible bloody war and to feel with all the wives, parents and children mourning for a beloved life.

SOURCES AND ADDITIONAL READING

Ayers P - *Women at War* - Liver Press 1988.

Bootle Times 1939 - 1945.

Borough of Bootle - *Proceedings of Council Volumes LVI - LXIV.*

Brookes R - *Never a Dull Moment* - Seal House Press 1968.

Calder A - *The People's War: Britain 1939 - 1945* - Panther 1969.

Cameron I - *Red Duster, White Ensign* - White Lion 1974.

Central Office of Information - *Front Line 1940-1941: The Official Story of Civil Defence 1942.*

Costello J & Hughes I - *The Battle of the Atlantic* - Collins 1977.

Crosby Herald 1939 - 1945.

Dunn C L (Ed) - *Medical History of the Second World War. Emergency Medical Services* - HMSO 1953.

Hay D - *The Merchant Navy 1939-1945: War Under the Red Ensign* - Janes Pub. Co. 1982.

Hyde F E - *Liverpool and the Mersey - An Economic History of a Port 1700 - 1970* - David and Charles 1971.

Jackson G - *History and Archaeology of Ports* - Worlds Work Ltd. 1983.

Jenkins J - *A History of Bootle* (unpublished).

Johnson A - *Working the Tides: Gatemen and Masters on the River Mersey* - Docklands History Project 1988.

Keegan J - *The Price of Admiralty: The Evolution of Naval Warfare* - Viking Penguin 1988.

Lane T - *Grey Dawn Breaking. British Merchant Seafarers in the late Twentieth Century* - Manchester University Press 1986.

Lane T - *The Merchant Seamen's War* - Manchester University Press 1990.

Lawton J - *A Veteran goes to War.* (unpublished).

Legal Proceedings - Bootle Borough.

Liddell Hart, BM - *History of the Second World War* - Cassell & Co., 1970.

Liverpool Daily Post and Echo - *Bombers over Merseyside: This was Merseyside's "finest hour". The authoritative record of the Blitz* - Scouse Press 1983.

Mersey Docks and Harbour Board - *Port at War, 1939 - 1945.* - MDHB 1946.

Mersey Docks and Harbour Board - *Port of Liverpool* - Historical Survey MDHB 1941.

Middlebrook M - *Convoy* - Penguin 1978.

Mountfield S - *Western Gateway* - A *History of the Mersey Docks and Harbour Board* - Liverpool University Press 1965.

O'Brien T H - *History of the Second World War - Civil Defence* - HMSO 1955.

Roskill S - *A Merchant Fleet in War: Alfred Holt & Co. 1939 - 1945* - Collins 1962.

Salmaggi C & Pallauisini A - *2194 Days of War* - A Mandadori 1977.

Salt Major G - *A History of Bootle in the Second World War* (unpublished).

Van der Vat D - *The Atlantic Campaign. The Great Struggle at Sea 1939 -1945* - Hodder and Stoughton 1988.

Wemyss D - *Relentless Pursuit* - William Kimber 1955.

Wemyss D - *Walker's Groups in the Western Approaches* - Liverpool Daily Post and Echo 1948.

Whitworth R - *Merseyside at War: Day-by-day diary of the 1940-1941 bombing* - Scouse Press 1988.

Individual Contributions

Bernard Baxter
George Bryson
Lionel Chappell
John Flaherty
Wilf G
Terry Gilligan
Frank H
Fred Hardy
Ced Hughes
May Logan
George Lunt
Albert and Mary Meadham
Bill Mower
Wally Riley
Dick Squires
Winifred Toale
Otto von Bulow
Harold Walker
Alf West